Personal Branding

How to Brand Yourself Online Using Social Media Marketing and the Hidden Potential of Instagram Influencers, Facebook Advertising, YouTube, Twitter, Blogging, and More

Contents

Introduction

This book is for anyone ready to master the art of personal branding in 2019 using social media and the many benefits that social media has to offer. If you are ready to "kill it" in the online space this year, then read on!

There is a lot out there regarding what it means to brand yourself personally, how personal branding works, and what you can achieve through your brand. Because of the rising popularity of the digital nomad lifestyle, everyone wants to learn how to brand themselves and build a network around themselves filled with people who are capable of helping them grow their brand. Naturally, this has led to a great deal of information floating around about how you can brand yourself, what is required for a personal brand, and what you need to do in order to turn your brand into one that converts. Of course, you do not want to waste your time sifting through seas of information when, in reality, you can just as easily read this guide and gain access to all of the most relevant and modern personal branding tools for 2019.

You must understand that each year, the methods used for branding and developing your business shift and evolve. What worked three years, two years, or even just a year ago, will not work as effectively now, in many cases, because the overall industry has developed to a point where it simply cannot continue to sustain outdated practices.

These days, virtually all online audiences are looking for a certain element of authenticity, personality, and expertise from anyone they choose to look up to. If you want to have a successful personal brand, you need to learn how you can develop these elements of your brand so that you can easily be discovered by anyone who may be trying to find a person who offers just what it is that you plan to offer.

If you are ready to discover the new age elements required for personal branding in 2019, and just how you can use these elements to develop a brand that will help you turn a profit, then it is time to begin your journey of developing your personal brand!

Dive in, and enjoy the process!

Chapter 1: The Personal Reality of Personal Branding

Before digging into the mechanisms of what it takes to develop a personal brand, first, it is a good idea to explore what a personal brand truly is so that you can decide whether or not you are ready to have one. Even if you already have a brand, if you are struggling to grow at the rate which you desire, reading this chapter will help you equip yourself with the right tools to approach your personal growth effectively. Personal branding is all the rage right now and, in one way or another, many people use it as a tool to develop their reputations and leverage their reputation to earn better opportunities in life. That being said, some people personally brand by leveraging their reputation to gain more in life, and people who brand as an intentional tool that helps them develop a profitable business. If you are reading this book, the chances are that you want to develop your very own profitable business by leveraging your brand, which is an incredible idea!

Before you get started, understanding what it takes out of you as a person to run your brand is important. Many people start their businesses with a lack of awareness regarding the development of their brand on a personal level. Of course, the way these particular brands develop is different from your average brand because they are based on you as a person, rather than a separate entity that you have developed for your brand itself. For that reason alone, there is plenty of personal work, commitment, and effort that goes into creating your brand. Ideally, you should be prepared to take on all of this personal work to allow yourself to grow into the fullest potential of your personal brand and truly make the most out of your efforts. In this chapter, you are going to explore what these things are, how they may impact you, and what you can do to ensure that you grow through them rather than find yourself feeling trapped or stuck under a difficult mountain of growth.

Keep Your Mind Open

When it comes to personal branding, you must keep an open mind if you are going to grow through all of the obstacles that you will face along the way. Personal branding may be straight forward on paper, but when it comes to applying what you have learned, you will need to discover how you can mentally stay on track to continue applying the steps day after day. For someone who has never been in branding before, it can take some time to "learn the ropes" and discover how you are going to get yourself out there and grow. For some people, developing a brand is largely about having freedom, which can lead to a lack of work ethic and an inability to stay committed, and for others, it is easy to stay focused and keep working away. If you find that you are someone who struggles to stay focused, you will need to keep your mind open to learn about new ways that you can continue applying yourself, even when it feels challenging to stay committed.

Another reason why you want to keep an open mind is that developing your brand can be challenging if you stay too attached to your original idea. You need to have a strong vision for what you want to create, while also remaining flexible in how it looks and the steps that you will take to get there. To put it simply, you do not know everything right now, and as you learn and develop your brand more, your vision will evolve over time. Keeping an open mind will allow you to continue developing your brand so that you can easily allow yourself to continue building without attempting to confine yourself to a dream that may no longer fit your needs or desires.

Always Focus on Your Personal Growth

When it comes to developing a personal brand, personal growth is important. People who follow you are going to be genuinely engaged in your personal growth journey, regardless of what industry you are in, because your growth will inspire their growth. The more you focus on your personal growth, the more you are going to show up for and serve your audience, which allows everyone to continue growing together. Do not be afraid to endure the growth that naturally arises on your path, as well as the growth that you feel called to explore along the way, as all forms of personal growth will only help you reinforce the power of your brand.

In addition to helping your audience relate with you and feel inspired, personal growth will also help you develop a stronger brand in general. When you continually work toward personal growth, your confidence and abilities increase as well, which makes it easier for you to continue showing up and serving your audience. Not only will your increased self-confidence support your brand, but it will also support your entire life in general as you can begin enjoying more of your life and more of yourself through your personal development.

Keep Your Goals Clear

When it comes to personal branding, it can be challenging to identify what parts of yourself should be associated with your visible brand and what parts should be kept to yourself. On the one hand, you want to stay authentic and share your true self with your audience, whereas on the other hand, you want to make sure that you are not confusing them by sharing too much or getting off-brand. The best way to make sure that you are always staying on-brand with your audience is to make sure that you are clear in the goals that you have with your personal brand. If you are interested in sharing your brand with your audience so that you can teach them about marketing, then make sure that all of the parts of your personal self that you share with them in one way or another pertains to marketing. If you are developing a health and wellness brand as a personal trainer, make sure that the visible elements of your brand all coincide with your health and wellness commitments. The clearer you are with your brand development, the easier it is going to be for you to know exactly what you should be sharing, and what you should not be sharing.

In addition to having goals for your brand, do not forget to have goals for yourself, too. When it comes to developing a personal brand, it can be easy to forget that you have other aspects of your life beyond the life that you are building around your brand in the online space. Having personal goals can keep you more active in your personal life so that you can continue developing as an individual alongside developing your brand, which will further improve your chances at success.

Give Yourself Permission to Evolve

When you develop a personal brand, it can be easy to grow attached to the image that you have developed for your brand and then struggle to allow yourself to evolve over time. Many people find themselves unwilling to evolve their brand because they fear that their audience will stop following them through the changes. The reality is actually quite different: virtually every personal brand evolves over time, and in most cases, all of their loyal followers will simply evolve with them and continue to support the brand through all of the different evolutions. Some of your audience may fall off along the way, but trust that as they fall off, even more aligned members from your audience will begin arriving for you to serve them.

It is important for your overall health that you allow evolution to be a necessary staple in your brand, as no one wants to remain the same forever. Attempting to remain the same forever will cause you to lose your authenticity, which will result in your brand falling apart and you losing interest in what it is that you are trying to develop. For some business owners, this can even become a point of significant mental stress as they no longer permit themselves to be who they are, but instead attempt to remain the same in order to serve their audience. Trust that your evolution is a valuable asset to your brand, and continue working toward your evolution consistently, while also allowing it to be an important part of the brand that you are developing. The more you work together with yourself and your audience through evolution, the more authentic your brand will stay along the way.

Be Willing to Learn New Things

A part of personal development and evolution is being willing to learn new things, and this is especially important when it comes to developing a brand. When you are developing a brand, make sure that you are open to learning all of the new elements that come with the process, such as the mindset and technical strategies that are required. Do not be afraid to put yourself out there and learn a new skill if it is going to help you develop your brand faster.

At first, much of what goes into developing a brand needs to be done by you—unless you plan on hiring people to support you with everything. Even still, you should be developing your brand for you, as developing it in any other way could result in your brand not coming across as authentic or interesting. If you want to increase your chances at being recognized by your target audience, learning how to develop your social media accounts, website, and message in general is vital. Not only is this going to help you develop your brand with your message, but it also empowers you to run your brand your way so that even if you cannot afford to hire anyone for help, you can still develop all of the working parts of your brand yourself. Do not be afraid to take courses, or read books like this one, on social media marketing and the like to support you in developing your brand in the online space.

Learn To Let Go

When it comes to developing your online brand, you also need to learn to let go. Letting go may be one of the most powerful tools that you learn when it comes to developing your personal brand, as it will allow you to keep your brand moving forward even in the face of adversity. Two of the most important times that you need to pay attention to letting go is when it comes to letting go of the things mean people say, and letting go of your need to be perfect. Criticism and perfectionism are two of the more challenging things to work through when it comes to developing your business, and learning to let go is a major key for allowing you to overcome both of these things.

Many people find that having criticism toward their brand is challenging because they feel like they are being attacked personally, which is rarely true. When it comes to criticism, you need to understand that in most cases, people are only criticizing your services, not you, and they are rarely criticizing you in a way that is intended to be harsh or mean. Instead, they are simply trying to provide you with feedback, and they may not necessarily have the skills required to provide positive feedback.

When it comes to letting go of perfectionism, this strategy is a powerful way to help you get your content out there sooner, rather than later. One thing that many people do is hold themselves back because they want everything to look perfect, which is rarely important to anyone other than themselves. Attempting to hold yourself up to standards of perfectionism can lead to you being afraid to move forward with anything because you will always be looking for flaws in your work. While you want to be proud of what you do, aim to have high standards, not perfect standards. Attempting to do everything perfectly will only result in you feeling as though you are not good enough, which may lead to you feeling unworthy of running your business. Do not be afraid to let go of perfectionism so that you can develop your business to the best of your abilities, and trust that your skills will evolve and improve as you grow.

Chapter 2: Clarifying Your Brand

Now that you are aware of what it will take from you as a person to develop your personal brand, it is time for you to get down to business! In this chapter, you are going to learn how to clarify your personal brand and start developing growth opportunities through actual technical growth strategies. If you are ready to really get growing and expand your business to meet its maximum potential, this chapter is an essential tool for you to get started.

Many people are unclear regarding what their personal brand truly is, or they are unclear on how they can effectively communicate their brand to another human because, to them, it just "is". When you develop a personal brand, it can be easy to forget that not everyone is you and that means that not everyone is going to truly understand what it is that you are creating, which can result in you feeling misunderstood. This becomes clear when people are attempting to develop a brand and no one is responding: the chances are that they are not being clear enough, so their audience is unaware of the fact that they are even their audience. If you are unable to communicate your brand with someone else clearly, you are going to have a hard time effectively building your brand to the point where other people will actually understand what it is that you are doing and then begin working with you.

Why Your Brand Needs to Be Clear

Brands are excellent tools that help companies reach their audience with products and services that fulfill their audience's needs. When it comes to developing a brand, your clarity is your superpower, as a clear brand can more effectively reach their target audience and provide them with the information, products, and services that they need. As you develop your brand, having a clear message will enable you to know not only what you are developing, but also how you should be working toward developing it. Since you have a very clear focus in mind, it should be easier for you to determine what your best course of action is as you grow, as you know exactly what you are working toward.

You want to work toward clarifying your brand on two levels: first, you need to clarify your brand to yourself so that you know what it is that you are working toward in your business, as mentioned. The second part of clarifying your brand, and that is equally as important, is clarifying it to your audience, as your audience is going to want to know precisely who you are and what they can expect from you. If you fail to clarify your brand to your audience, your audience may fail to understand what it is that you are, and also fail to recognize that they are your audience, or they may fail to see the significance in your brand and how it impacts them. To avoid this, you need to identify how you can clarify your brand to yourself and your audience so that you are both always operating on the same page.

Clarifying Your Brand Goal

The next step in developing your clarified brand is identifying what your overall brand goal is. If you already have one of these, you can simply revisit your existing brand goal and ensure that it has been developed with enough clarity and purpose to support you in developing your brand. If you have not yet developed a brand goal, you want to clarify one single brand goal that is essentially the primary thing that you are working toward. This primary goal ensures that you have a very clear focus concerning what direction you are taking your brand in, which will allow you to develop the rest of your clarity around your personal brand.

Creating a brand goal is rather simple: you just need to identify what your mission is and why it is your mission, and then you have a brand goal! Ideally, your brand goal should be straightforward and directed on one very specific outcome to ensure that you are always working toward something that is easy to identify. Attempting to highlight an elaborate brand goal is only going to result in you feeling a lack of focus and understanding around what it is that you are trying to pursue.

Here are some examples of brand goals from popular brands that you have likely come across at some point in your life, to give you an idea of what an effective brand goal looks like:

- *Brand Power*: helping people purchase high-quality products with confidence.
- *Mr. Clean*: making cleaning easier.
- *Coca-Cola*: bringing people together to enjoy each other's company.
- *Dr. Oz*: educating people on natural health practices, and how they can take their wellbeing into their own hands.
- *Special K*: providing tasty, healthier snacks, and breakfast food items.

By clearly identifying what outcome you want your audience to have from your brand, you make it easier for you to work toward something specific. You should spend a few minutes thinking about what your goal is, and then seek to summarize your brand's goal in a single sentence. If you can narrow your goal down to just one sentence, then you know that you have clarified it enough to be able to stay laser-focused on what it is that you desire to accomplish.

It is important to understand that your brand is going to have different types of goals along the way, but your primary goal will always remain the same. Other goals you may experience include ones such as how many clients you would like to book, how you want to increase your follower ratio, and other similar goals. These types of goals are better described as being milestone goals that are set to help you achieve your overall goal. While these goals are equally as important, they do not identify what it is that you are working toward but instead identify how you are going to work toward it and what milestones need to be made for you to identify that you are clearly working toward your bigger goal.

Highlighting Your Core Values

In addition to highlighting your brand's primary goal, you also want to highlight your brand's core values, as your core values are going to help you highlight the clear path toward your goal. After all, there are many ways that any particular goal can be achieved, yet there is one specific way that should be pursued to help your path remain on-track with your brand overall. Your core values will ensure that your chosen path toward your goal always aligns with what your brand stands for and cares about. Your audience cares about your core values because often they want to connect with brands who share similar core values so that they feel confident they are going to be served in a way that relates to their needs on many levels.

Highlighting your brand's core values is simple: you only want to choose two. Ideally, these two core values should complement one another so that they both support you in advancing toward greater success in your business. You can use any two core brand values, though ideally, you want to be using core values that resonate with you and your audience to ensure that you are working toward that which your audience actually cares about. It is also important that you relate with your core values; otherwise, you are going to have difficulty connecting with your audience, and you will find yourself being ignored as you attempt to market your brand.

The easiest way to identify your core values when you are representing your brand is first to identify your personal core values, as this is going to help you choose values that you truly care about. If your personal core values reflect well with your brand and support your audience as well, then you might consider leading with these. Alternatively, you might want to use your own core values to help you carve out what matters to you so that you can choose ones relating to your brand and that are still going to resonate with you, while also serving your brand.

After you have highlighted your brand's core values, pay attention to how these core values resonate with your overall goal. See if you can identify an ideal path toward achieving your goal using your core values so that you can clearly create the outcome that you desire using a process that supports you in staying aligned with your brand values. For example, maybe your goal is to help moms get fit, and your values are placed with harmony and kids. So, you want to highlight a way for moms to get fit using strategies that are harmonious with their busy work schedules and that places value on the kids, perhaps by incorporating the kids into the workouts. Right now, you do not need to highlight your entire path to success using these three pieces of information, but having them available allows you to ensure that you are focused and that any steps you take toward achieving your business goals are on-brand.

It is important to understand that, just as with goals, you can absolutely have more than two values—this simply means that you are only going to have two core values that you work toward with your business. The rest of the values that you have will matter, but at the end of the day, these are the two values that you will measure everything by to ensure that you are staying focused on your brand's true purpose. In most cases, you can honor your values, but this way, if there is ever action that you need to take where your values begin to conflict with one another, you know that you need to work on behalf of your core values, not your secondary values.

Refining Your Existing Brand

Since you are creating a personal brand, it is inevitable that you already have a brand in place as your personal brand is simply your reputation. The chances are that you have already attempted to define your brand and use it toward generating success, too, so you now desire to simply refine your brand so that you can develop it even further. If you are just starting out, you may only now be learning how to take your personal brand into your own hands for your growth. Or, if you have been doing this for a while, you may be looking into how you can refine your existing brand so that you can actually begin developing profits, allowing you to make it all worth it. In any case, learning how to refine your brand essentially means releasing all of the things that do not serve your brand and laser focusing in on what it is exactly you are trying to create, and how you can create it with your personal brand. This way, you can begin developing your brand with an even clearer focus and working toward serving your audience in a more refined way so that you can increase your success. Remember: the more focused and clear you are with how you are serving, the easier it is for you to serve your audience and develop your profits through your brand.

When it comes to refining a brand that already exists, one of the most useful tools that you can take advantage of is learning how to look through the brand that you have already built to identify where your core message lies. When you look back through your existing content, it becomes easier for you to see what you talk about most, what your values are, and how you can help people in the best way possible. The benefit here is that you also gain the opportunity to see how your audience has already been responding to what you have been putting out so that you can identify whether or not they actually resonate with what you have been sharing. This way, as you develop your clarified brand, you can also decide whether or not your brand reflects well on your audience.

If you begin looking through the engagement that you have already been receiving and find that you are not getting consistent engagement, or you are not getting consistent engagement from people who are a part of your target audience, you can refine differently. In this way, rather than attempting to understand what your audience likes and what they want more of, you can begin understanding why your target audience is not yet responding to your content. This way, you can begin adjusting your message so that your audience really resonates with what you are saying and begins responding to the content that you are putting out.

Summarizing Your Brand

After you have gone through the process of setting goals and outlining your core values, you want to begin summarizing your brand overall. In the process of identifying your goal and values, you identified your why and how, so now you want to identify your who, or what. You can identify what your brand is, or whom your brand persona is, by focusing on summarizing your brand in approximately five words. The more you fill out your who, what, why, and how, the easier it is going to be for you to communicate your brand and brand messages to your audience as you practice sharing your marketing strategies. As you begin to identify the who or what of your brand, you really want to get deeper into the consideration of what your actual identity is, as this is where you are going to find your "who".

When it comes to identifying your who, do not make it larger or more complex than it needs to be: identifying your brand in five words or less is the best way to ensure that you stay clear and focused. Here, you do not need to identify anything beyond "who". So, for example, Coca-Cola may identify as "A soda company" or Nike may identify as "A fashionable athletic wear company." These are simple, direct, and focused descriptions of what your brand is, making it easier for you to understand what it is that you are creating.

Creating A Brand Board

Now that your brand has been clarified in terms of who, what, why, and how, you may want to start developing an image for your brand through a brand board. Brand boards, sometimes called mood boards, are a powerful tool that many brands use to identify what the overall aesthetic is that they want to design for their brand itself. Having a brand board as a part of your clarification process is a valuable way to ensure that you are keeping your aesthetic on-brand with your overall image, which allows you to stay focused on how you are conveying your brand. The more you focus on developing a clear message, combined with a clear aesthetic, the more you are going to be able to grow overall as your brand will progressively grow more attractive to others due to the clarity. Remember: the biggest value that clarity provides you with is a clear understanding of what it is that you have to offer so that your audience knows exactly why you are so significant to them and why they need to follow you to gain what you have to offer.

Brand boards can easily be created on a platform like Pinterest, or you can print out your brand board images and paste them on a piece of cardboard like a vision board. Creating a branding board will allow you to get clear on what colors, fonts, and image types you want to have associated with your brand. As you are building, make sure that you are putting together an image that is coherent and that makes sense to ensure that you are designing a brand that people can understand. Attempting to weave together too many different colors, fonts, or aesthetics can result in your brand losing clarity, which results in you losing the value of clarifying your brand.

Once you have developed your brand board, all you need to do is allow yourself to compare your marketing materials against your brand board to ensure that you are creating materials that make sense to your brand. Seek always to maintain similar elements, colors, and aesthetics to ensure that you are developing a brand that makes sense. If you find that you begin making marketing materials that do not compare to your brand board in any way, do not be afraid to update your materials to ensure that they fit your brand board. If you find that you are consistently developing materials that are not on-brand, do not be afraid to adjust your brand board to fit your new aesthetic. Ideally, your brand board should be used as a tool that keeps you on-track—it should not feel like you are taking anything away from the brand that you feel naturally called to create, especially since the brand that you are creating revolves around you as a person.

The final element to using a brand board as a tool is reviewing it every quarter, as your brand board will need updating alongside evolving marketing trends. As marketing continues to develop new trends and styles for what is relevant and how you can reach your audience best, evolving your brand board to reflect that is important. The more you focus on keeping your brand board up to date and trending, the easier it will be for you to develop a brand that is going to stay relevant to your audience.

Chapter 3: Online and Local Influencers

Influencers are one of the hottest marketing tools available in the modern marketplace, especially online, as influencers can get your brand in front of an existing audience. Influencers hold so much power because their entire focus is around developing an audience in a specific niche industry and gaining the trust, affection, and appreciation of that audience. As a result, when they market products or services to that audience, or even introduce a new individual to that audience, that product, service, or individual gains a lot of attention immediately. Essentially, they are professionally endorsing said product, service, or individual to their audience, which is ultimately what the influencer's primary goal is in their job. As a result of their status and recognition, influencers get paid a healthy income for endorsing products, which allows them to continue developing their platform even larger, in turn making them even more valuable to other brands.

As you develop your brand, influencers can help you in many different ways. One way that an influencer can support you is by endorsing you as a person, likely by connecting with you and sharing images of you or giving a "shout out" to you on social media. Another way, or the more likely way, is by having an influencer experience your products or services firsthand so that they can tell their audience how much they like your products or services. This is often done in exchange for a commission that they receive each time their audience purchases one of your products from having seen it being endorsed by the influencer. You will learn more about how influencers work in this chapter, and how you can approach an influencer and begin working with one so that you can increase your growth on social media.

How Influencer's Work

You are probably not new to the world of influencers, especially if you have been on the internet for even five minutes in the last five years. Influencers are a unique form of social media "star" that developed their platforms as a way to help brands get their products or services to more customers, by leveraging the influencer's platform. Basically, a true influencer's primary purpose is to generate a massive buzz online and get well known for being themselves, while they target a very specific audience. Typically, they will target an audience that mirrors one that a certain industry would want to tap into, such as young fashion, makeup, or the health and wellness industry. By targeting a relevant audience and developing a huge following in that niche, influencers become valuable assets to companies as they can get a company's product or service seen by the very people who are most likely to buy it. Because the influencer has spent so much time developing their audience and growing these relationships, the influencer no longer has to earn their trust, which means that nearly anything they recommend is immediately more appealing to their audience. Their audience already knows that the influencer will not lie to them about the quality of a product; therefore, they know that if the said influencer is endorsing it, it must be good. If an influencer were to lie in exchange for a deal with a paying brand, that influencer would lose their audience's trust, which would, in turn, destroy their business growth. That being said, the number one priority for an influencer is to earn and maintain the trust of their audience.

These days, the idea of being able to get paid for endorsing cool new products is really popular, which means that many people are trying to get in front of an audience and establish themselves as an influencer. What has happened is that many people are finding the influencer field to be swamped with false influencers or people who only have a couple of thousand followers yet still claim that they are capable of turning a large profit for a company. While growth is to be expected, and to achieve a larger status means to start smaller, many of these wannabe influencers do not realize how much work and devotion it takes actually to become a true influencer. As a result, they fall off the face of the map and remain completely pointless for brands to work with. As a brand yourself, you want to learn to avoid associating with anyone who is not a true influencer, as this can result in you investing far too much into people who cannot truly provide you with the value that you need from an influencer.

The flip side of the influencer industry is low-quality brands who are trying to profit off of influencers or wannabe influencers. This side of the industry creates havoc in two ways: through spamming true influencers, and through profiting off of those who wish they were true influencers. As a brand yourself, you do not want to identify with either of these categories as it can lead to you being seen as a low-quality brand with virtually nothing to offer, which can potentially destroy your credibility. If you were to excessively spam true influencers in order to attempt to cut a deal with them, especially if you are approaching it in an unethical way, you might find your brand being seen as spam in general. The result of this behavior can be influencers seeing you as being a low-quality brand, which can quickly spread through the industry, leading to people no longer respecting you or wanting to work with you. As a result, you lose access to this valuable tool, resulting in your brand missing out due to your irresponsible approach to these professionals.

The other half of this is approaching wannabe influencers or people who are not truly influencers, such as those who only have a few hundred or a couple thousand followers, and asking them to be an influencer for your brand. This is a common phenomenon between brands who are trying to make a quick sale, so they essentially butter up a person's ego by leading them to believe that they have the potential to be an influencer. Often, these brands will request that said "influencer" purchase certain products or services from them, and in exchange, they will receive a promo code to share with their followers. In this case, the brand actually profits more off of the wannabe influencers than they do off of the people whom the influencer sends their way, which is the whole point overall. Although this may result in profits for the brand, it can also result in the brand being seen as not genuine, low quality, and unworthy, making it harder for the brand to grow in any meaningful way.

Finding Influencers Online

There are two types of influencers that you may want to work with: those who are online and who have a massive global audience, or those who are local and have a massive local audience. Ideally, you should be tapping into both types of influencers, even if your brand is exclusively online and lacks any true local element to it. Tapping into global influencers will give you massive recognition, helping you really turn more eyes on your company, which gives you the capacity to increase your overall earning potential. If you are an online brand or a brand with an online element, this is also the best way for you to begin getting your brand out there so that people can find you and begin purchasing your products.

The best way to begin finding influencers is to start searching your industry online on social media platforms and search engines. Start by paying attention to who the major influencers in your industry are, and really focus on how they nurture their audience and what allows them to be so effective and successful at what they do. The more you grow to understand the most successful influencers in your industry, the more you can identify which influencers are going to be the most effective for you to work with. The chances are, early on, you will not be able to effectively work a deal with the most successful influencer as you may not be able to afford it or they may not be interested in working with someone who has yet to develop a significant following in their business. However, you will be able to work with influencers who are still carrying a significant impact and who see the potential in your business. For you to qualify them to ensure that your connection would be mutually beneficial, you will want to ensure that you are comparing them against the more successful influencers in your industry. This way, you can guarantee that you are working with influencers who have high potential and are capable of getting your name out there.

Great places to look for influencers include on Twitter's trending tab, Instagram's discovery page or any top post page for hashtags associated with your niche, and in influential Facebook groups. You can also find influencers by simply going to Google and keying in "famous (industry) influencers". This is an excellent way for you to start finding people in your niche who are effectively targeting your audience so that you can get discovered by a larger number of people even faster.

Finding Influencers Locally

If you want to begin connecting with local influencers, you can do so by using all of the same search techniques as you used with global influencers, but including location-specific search parameters. Typically, the easiest way to find local influencers is to look at the "top posts" section of an Instagram hashtag search for a local hashtag, which enables you to begin identifying who is popular in your area. Then, you simply need to begin looking for those who appear to be a part of your niche so that you can start interacting with them. You can begin by following them and jotting down their names somewhere so that you know which influencers were the ones that were local to you, as opposed to the rest which may not necessarily be local at all.

Even if you are not a strictly local business, having access to local influencers is a powerful opportunity for you to begin working together with local influencers to maximize your audience. With local influencers, you can begin to cultivate true in-person friendships and potentially even be seen with these influencers locally, which allows you to snap pictures with them and tag them in your local images. This is a great opportunity, as well, for you to have people who are nearby who understand the industry that you are in and who can become genuine friends with you. As you may recall from Chapter 1, having people who understand you and can enjoy this part of your life with you is a great opportunity for you to continue enjoying your industry without feeling any isolation that is occasionally experienced by entrepreneurs. So, developing your local influencer circle is not only valuable for your brand but for your overall wellbeing, too.

Ethically Connecting with Influencers

Once you have identified the influencers that you would like to connect with, you must not connect until you understand how to do so ethically and compassionately. Remember: influencers work with brands all the time, which means that they are used to collaborating with brands who are professional and know how to approach them professionally and charismatically. Spamming their feed and asking them questions on their comment section is not going to charm an influencer into believing that you are the one they need to work with, as this looks unprofessional and juvenile. Ideally, you should be approaching influencers professionally and gracefully, which allows them to see you as respectful, and makes them more likely to want to do business with you. If you are blasting their wall with spam and attempting to create a superficial friendship between yourself and an influencer, all you are going to find is that they see you as being fake and they develop a bad taste for who you are and what you have to offer. If you start off this way, you will find, over time, that the influencer will not talk to you even if you offer a respectable approach because they are not interested in your fake attention. They may even think of you as unstable or potentially risky to do business with, leaving them especially cautious around you.

When it comes to approaching an influencer ethically, you should focus on doing so by first learning more about them. Follow the influencer for a week or two, casually engage with their content, and get a feel for who they truly are. Do not get overwhelmed or lost in their follower numbers and their image, as you want to ensure that you have a feel for who they are as a person—since this is a person who is about to be representing you in your business should you two strike a deal. You want to pick people who are going to represent you in a positive and powerful way, allowing you to gain maximum growth from your connection with the said influencer.

After you have followed them for a few days or a week, take your time to see if they are actually going to be a good fit for your business. Then, if you decide that they are, you can begin the process of making contact with them to see if they are interested in doing business with you. Typically, a professional influencer will have some form of information available on their platforms as to how you should go about contacting them if you want to do business with them. If you do see a point of contact, you will want to use this to get in touch with the influencer to ensure that you approach them in the way that they prefer. A good way to show your respect is to respect how they wish to be approached, so do not skip this crucial first step by messaging them in any other way. If the influencer does not have an established point of contact, you can always reach out to them through their private messages to see if they want to offer you a point of contact for you to connect with them. This initial message should be brief, as all you want to do is introduce yourself and your purpose for messaging them, and then ask if they would be interested in further connecting over a potential deal together. If they answer you, follow the instructions that they send you to begin creating the deal that you want to create with your chosen influencer.

As you begin to engage in conversations with the influencer of your choice, make sure that you are professional and polite the entire way, as you are engaging in a business deal. While you can certainly be friendly, you want to ensure that you do not begin acting exclusively as friends as you will need to maintain the professional end of this to create an effective business deal with the influencer. If you have never worked with an influencer before, you may benefit from asking the influencer what their typical approach to working together with brands is so that you can get a feel for how they generally work with others. If they say that it is up to you, then you need to decide what you want to offer the influencer, including what products or services you will give them and what commission you will pay them in exchange for their endorsement. The commission is typically structured in one of three ways: you pay them for their post, you pay them per sale they make, or you offer them product credit per sale they make. Understand that the more professional and influential the influencer is, the more they are going to expect to be paid per deal to ensure that they are getting paid their worth. You need to be prepared to meet the influencer where they are at or offer to reach out to them again later on when you have better finances to support the higher fee they require.

Creating Deals with Influencers

After you have approached an influencer with a potential deal and have reached a point of agreement where you are both ready to begin officially working together, some important steps need to take place to ensure that you and the influencer are both protected. The biggest key here is making sure that your agreement is very clear, that every aspect is discussed and agreed upon, and that you turn the agreement into an official work order contract that you both sign. Having an official contract between the two of you ensures that you are both protected, by legally binding you to pay the agreed-upon fee and the influencer to perform the agreed-upon marketing services. If either of you defaults, the other is allowed to back out of the agreement, or uphold any terms that may have been fixed in the agreement.

There are many sample agreements available online that you can use to begin working out professional contracts with influencers so that you can operate professionally and protect both of your interests in the agreement. Find the one that best suits the agreement that you have made, ensure that the information in the agreement is relevant to you and the influencer, and then sign it and ensure that you both keep a signed copy.

Once the agreement has been created, you need to get to work on completing your part of the agreement. This may mean sending a product or fulfilling a service for the influencer so that they can begin reviewing the product or service at their agreed-upon time. It is important that you are timely with this fulfillment so that the influencer can get to work on your deal—they are not going to want to wait for you. In fact, they may even have a clause that states that they are free to back out of the agreement if they find that you have taken too long to fulfill your end of the deal. Either way, to respect the influencer that you are working with and protect your chances at working with them and other influencers in the future, being timely and professional is important.

Following the fulfillment of this part of your agreement, you need to ensure that you fulfill any other steps as well. Again, stay professional and make sure that you keep up to date with the influencer at all times so that the communication remains open. The more that you both stay on the same page and approach your agreement together, the more fluid the agreement will be fulfilled and the easier it will be for you to gain your benefits from the influencer. Moreover, the easier you are to work with, the more likely the influencer is going to want to work with you again, or recommend you to other influencers who may be interested in working with your brand. Remember: you are working with someone who is literally hired to review you professionally, so you need to be on your best behavior so that you can be reviewed positively.

Chapter 4: Facebook and Instagram

Leveraging Instagram influencers is a powerful way to get in front of your target audience, but if you really want to make a big impact, you are also going to want to develop your own platform so that people who find you through an influencer can follow you on their own. Ideally, this will help you build up a significant presence so that you can stop leveraging influencers as frequently, or instead use them to scale your existing profits so that you can grow even larger. Developing your presence online will also add some credibility to your brand, as people tend to trust those with an established presence more than they do those who have no presence at all. In this chapter, you are going to learn about how you can develop a strong Facebook and Instagram presence so that you can have a platform available for your audience to look to as they begin to discover your brand.

Why Develop Facebook and Instagram Together?

Facebook and Instagram are interconnected, as Facebook bought out Instagram in 2013 and has been developing the two platforms alongside each other ever since. When you are building a professional presence on one of these platforms, it always pays to have one on the other platform as well so that you can combine the efforts of both platforms and develop your presence even further. Typically, most brands will favor one platform over the other, although they will tend to see positive benefits from having both platforms in action.

When you choose to launch an Instagram business account, you are required to have a Facebook business page to link it to so that Instagram can draw on information about your business from Facebook's platform. If you do not already have a business page on Facebook, you will be prompted to make one when you choose to convert your Instagram page to a business page. If you want to develop a professional presence and broaden your reach, you are going to want to have a business profile on both Facebook and Instagram, as business profiles offer plenty of additional support beyond basic profiles.

On Facebook, a business page allows you to create a complete in-depth profile for your business that provides your potential audience with plenty of information about your business. Your page can include information such as the name and location of your business, ways to contact you, how your business was founded, and what your business offers. It can also offer unique features such as the ability to share video content, a selling platform so that you can sell products directly from Facebook, and a services tab that shows your visitors what services you offer. You can use as many of these features as you see fit for your business to enable you to have access to even more ways to serve your audience directly from Facebook itself. Even if this will not be your primary platform, having all of these features filled out and made available is a great opportunity to grow your platform even further.

Beyond the intricacy of details made available on Facebook, you can also use Facebook to develop paid advertisements for both platforms. Facebook is where both Facebook and Instagram paid advertisements are hosted, so you can use your business account to create an ads manager and then leverage those ads to help you begin developing an even bigger audience on both platforms. If you want to advertise special products, services, sales, launches, or anything else, having a Facebook business account with an ads manager is important.

Instagram offers another great business profile option that is typically more interactive and social for most people. Instagram tends to be where followers are more likely to interact, and it is also known for being easier to attract new followers due to the usage of hashtags and geotags. Furthermore, the audience on Instagram is generally more receptive of personal brands and will often be more likely to discover you and show support to you as a personal brand. With a business profile, Instagram will operate in virtually the same way as personal profiles will, except that they also enable the opportunity to see your profile's analytics. So, you will be able to track how many people are paying attention to your posts, stories, and IGTV shares so that you can begin to identify what content your audience loves the most and what they are not so fond of. This way, you know what you can create more of and how you can continue serving your audience.

Instagram is also beneficial as it offers the opportunity to share your Instagram posts to your Facebook business page, meaning that you can manage a great deal of your organic marketing on Facebook from your Instagram page. As you build an online presence, you will likely find that this integration is valuable as it operates as a time saver to give you plenty of content without having to create so much. As a result, Facebook and Instagram work great together to manage both paid and organic marketing back and forth, making it easy to develop both of these platforms at the same time and with minimal efforts.

While you could consider operating just one or the other, it does not make sense to in the modern world. Studies done in 2018 showed that at least 75 percent of millennials check either Facebook or Instagram to try and find a business online, as this is how they can see the popularity and reputation of the business. If they cannot find a business on either of these platforms, typically, they will not do business with the said business because they feel that this minimizes their credibility.

Developing A Facebook Business Page

Developing a business page on Facebook is rather simple—all you need to do is go to the "Create A Page" feature on the left side action menu on your desktop and then begin the creation process. First, you will be walked through the process of choosing your page name, which, ideally, should be your business name. Then, you also want to create a profile picture and a header image for your page. Since this is your professional page, choose a professional profile image and a header image that is relevant to your brand, and reflects your business positively in one way or another.

From this point forward, you can use all of the following tips to optimize your Facebook page whether or not you already have one. So, if you are just starting out, use this guidance to develop your page, and if you have had your page for a while, use this guidance to ensure that your page is optimized for your unique brand.

Customize Your Username

Every page has a username, and you are going to want to create one for your page as well. You should set your username to one that is the same as what you use on other platforms so that you can easily be found on Facebook as well. People will then be able to search for your username in the search bar on Facebook and find you there.

Create A Call to Action

On Facebook, there is a call-to-action feature that you can use on your page, which allows you to encourage people to engage in a certain activity on your page. For example, you might have a "Sign Up" or "Message" button. You want to take advantage of this call to action, as it prompts people to further engage with your business when they land on your page. You can use whatever button feature you think is going to help you convert more followers into clients through Facebook.

Customize Your Page Tabs

On Facebook, tabs are features on a page that enable you to share specific pieces of information with your audience. You can use whatever tabs resonate with your business format most, from online shopping features to review tabs or even video tabs. Facebook has plenty of built-in tabs that you can use and customize to offer a more enriching experience for your audience. There are also custom tab creators that you can use that enable you to create custom tabs that you can then "plugin" to your Facebook page so that your audience can have an even more personalized experience with your brand. If you are not tech-savvy, but you have an idea for a custom tab, you can always consider hiring someone from Fiverr to help you generate your tab.

All Facebook pages come with some standard tabs already turned on, so as you are customizing your tab features, do not be afraid to turn the ones that you are not using off. Having tabs turned on that you are not using can make your page look incomplete, so you want to hide these by turning these tab styles off.

Categorize Your Page Properly

Every Facebook page can be placed into a specific category that will tell followers what type of page they are following. You want to make sure that you categorize your page properly so that people are clear about what you are and what you have to offer. Moreover, if you connect your Facebook page to your Instagram page, your category will be shown on Instagram so you can use this as an additional tool on Instagram to immediately show people who and what you are.

Leverage Influencer Content

When it comes to developing your platform on Facebook, you can leverage influencer content that you have generated from influencers elsewhere. For example, if an influencer posts a picture featuring your products on Instagram, you can share that image to your Facebook page and tag the influencer in it, then encourage people to head over to their Instagram page to grab a custom promo code for your page. This is a great way to cross-promote influencers, gain the most out of your work together, and also make yourself more enjoyable and valuable to work with so that, over time, influencers want to work with you even more.

In addition to deals that you have struck with influencers, you can use user-generated content to help you begin promoting your products or services as well. For example, if one of your followers shares an image of them using your products or services, you can share that picture to your Facebook page and tag them. This is a great way to get in front of their audience while sharing them with yours, and growing your reach. User-generated content is a highly popular category of content for business pages, so do not be shy about using this type of content. If you get people who have a wonderful image and a fairly significant following, this can be a great opportunity for you to get in front of their audience even more and create a sense of community between your brand and clients.

Creating Organic Content

On Facebook, you can develop organic content in whatever way you want to. You can do this by simply sharing Instagram updates to Facebook, or you can begin creating content for Facebook itself. Most brands will do both, although some who do not prefer the Facebook platform may stick exclusively to Instagram and let their Instagram content carry their Facebook page.

If you do want to create content specifically for Facebook, there are plenty of content styles that you can create for the platform. One type of content that you can create are actual status updates, ranging from 150 characters to 500 characters, filled with information that is relevant to your industry or business. If you choose to create status updates, unless they are extremely short, you should include an image with them as visual advertising is trending more and more each year, which means that including pictures makes your content more likely to get seen. You can also share pictures without status updates, or with minimal status updates. Often, companies will do this using quotes or memes that are used to provide their audience with something entertaining or inspiring, and relevant to their niche. Another great share is videos, either ones that you have made or ones that you have enjoyed and find to be relevant, as video marketing is trending as well. Many companies are using live video features as a way to share exclusive moments with their audience so that they can begin developing positive relationships with their audience. Beyond that, you can share other people's posts, other websites, or virtually anything else that you find interesting and relevant to your audience.

If you do choose to share content from others, make sure that you keep this content to 40 percent or less of the overall content you share. Since you are a personal brand, you want to keep most of your content organic and personally created to avoid driving all of your hard-earned traffic to other people's platforms. If you share too much of other people's content, they may think that these other people are more interesting and that you are simply a place they can go to learn about other brands. In other words, you can drive your traffic away from you and lose the quality of your audience, and minimize your personal conversions.

Leveraging Facebook Advertisements

Facebook is the platform that you will go to when you want to create paid advertisements, whether you plan on posting them on Facebook, Instagram, or both. Facebook's ad manager account offers an in-depth opportunity for you to create the entire front and back end of your advertisements, allowing you to control everything from how they look to who sees them and how much they cost you.

Ideally, you want to establish a healthy organic audience before you begin paying for your advertisements, as you want to make sure that the audience you are marketing to is actually going to be the audience most likely to purchase from you. That way, you are not paying to run advertisements to a segment of your industry that is not going to end up paying you anything. You can easily establish a healthy organic audience over three-six months and then begin using the analytics from that audience to input demographic information into your ads manager so that you can advertise to your audience effectively.

Once you have established your audience, running advertisements on Facebook is simple. You will start by going to your business page and then tapping the "Promote" tab at the top of the page. This will take you to a page where you can tap "Ads Manager", which will then take you to the actual ads manager itself. There, you can click "New Ad" and begin creating the new advertisement that you want to begin promoting.

You will start by choosing the type of ad that you want to create, and then the objective. Facebook offers plenty of objectives that you can choose from, so consider what your goal is with your advertisement and then choose an objective that will be respective to that goal. Once you have, you can begin following the next steps, such as defining who your audience is, where your ad will be placed, and what your budget is going to be. You can also set the schedule for how long your ad is going to run for, and how much you want to pay per day or impression. Next, you want to begin creating the design for your ad by choosing what picture you want to be associated with the ad, what words you are going to use, and what you want people to do when they see your ad. You will have a call to action button featured on your ad that encourages people to do something such as "buy", "sign up" or "learn more".

After you have set up all of these elements of your advertisement, you can go ahead and click "Confirm". Facebook will then run your ad through a program that ensures that your page is sharing no vulgar language or inappropriate photograph. This way, they can ensure that Facebook stays family-friendly and that you are not violating any terms of agreement on their platform. Once they have approved your ad as being appropriate for the platform, they will begin running it. This typically only takes a few minutes up to a couple of hours.

An alternative promotional style that you can use on Facebook is known as "boosted posts". These are simple: all you do is go to a post that you would like to promote, tap "Boost Post" and then follow the prompts on the screen. You will have the opportunity to identify your audience, set your budget, and then set your schedule for how long you want to promote the post for. These types of promotions are great if you have a post that is performing well and that you would like to see perform even better or attract new audience members to your audience so that more people become aware of your brand. Ideally, you should use a mix between promotions and boosted posts so that you can begin getting your page even further out there, allowing you to grow more consistently on Facebook.

Developing an Instagram Business Page

Developing an Instagram business page is significantly easier than developing a Facebook business page because Instagram offers far fewer customizable features for you to adjust on your platform. Although this does mean that your followers will not have quite as much information as your Facebook followers will, it also means that getting your profile set up is much easier. You can set up an Instagram profile from your mobile phone in just a few minutes and have it completely branded and ready to be shared with your audience.

If you already have an Instagram page, you can use this guide to help you optimize your page so that it is properly branded for you and your audience. If you do not already have an Instagram page, follow these steps to get yours set up. Before you do, however, go into your

Instagram's profile settings and tap "Switch to Business Account" so that you can connect your Instagram profile to a Facebook business page and begin accessing all of Instagram's business features.

Branding your Instagram page has five steps: your profile image, your username, your bio, your website, and your story highlights. You will also use your newsfeed itself, but that is detailed in the next section. In the meantime, below, you can find information on how all of the features mentioned above can be branded to improve the quality of your account.

Profile Image

Your profile image needs to be something attractive, clear, and minimal when it comes to Instagram. Having an unclear profile image, any type of filter on it, or too many details going on will result in your profile image being confusing to your audience. On Instagram, profile pictures are small and cannot be zoomed in or enlarged, so you need to keep that in mind and choose something professional, clean, and easy to understand. If you are a personal brand, this should be an image of your face that reflects your brand well; otherwise, you might consider using a logo or a clean image of your product. Avoid using stock images or anything of the sort, as this can make your profile have a fake or inauthentic feel to it.

Username

Your username should be simple to remember, on-brand, and clear. Having a username that is not clear or easy to spell can result in your audience wondering who you are, difficulty finding you again, or otherwise thinking you may not be authentic. You should keep your username the same as a username that you may be using for your brand anywhere else online, as keeping all of your platforms connected to the same username makes discovering you online significantly easier.

Bio

On Instagram, you have a short 150-character bio that you can use to describe your brand and encourage people to follow you. You must use this bio effectively to ensure that you are giving your audience a clear description of who you are and what they can expect when following you. Your bio does not need to be large or complex. Some companies use something simple like "Clean burning soy wax candles." Others use something more personal, like "24 / Gemini / Travel / Play." You will want to create something that resonates with you, tells your audience what to expect when following you, and gives them an idea of what they need to be sticking around for.

If you are unsure about how you can create your bio, you can always look at other personal brands and get a feel for what they have created. Sometimes, seeing other people's bios can inspire you to create your own so that you are designing one that is actually interesting and attractive. That being said, do not directly copy someone else's bio as this can take away from your own authenticity and credibility and result in people not wanting to follow you anymore.

Website

Instagram lets you link your website to your profile, so you must take advantage of that. You can use this link in a few ways, such as the following:

- Link to your homepage on your website
- Link to your current special offer
- Link to another popular platform you use (like YouTube or Podcasts)
- Link to a landing page like Link Tree so that you can lead people to various platforms (i.e., a landing page that leads people to YouTube, your website, your latest special, etc.)

Story Highlights

On Instagram, a great branding feature that you can take advantage of are story highlights. Story highlights can be used by simply choosing a story that you like and then categorizing it as a highlight on your page. Many brands will use story highlights to offer fun long-term information for their audience so that their audience can get a more personalized feel for whom they are following. For example, a make-up artist might use a story highlight tab to share looks and one to share tutorials. A health coach might use story highlights to share certain workout routines, health tips, and simple recipes or food inspiration for people to use. A travel blogger might have a different story highlight for some of their favorite trips so that they can share their experiences. You can customize your story highlights however you want and leverage them for your brand's growth. The main key here is that you take advantage of them and regularly share so that your audience can thumb through your highlights and consume even more from you when they find your page. In this day and age, followers love consuming content from the people they love, so having plenty of content for an excited new follower to consume can help them establish a memory of you in their mind so that they remember you and pay attention more frequently.

Leveraging Instagram Organic Marketing

Developing organic marketing content on Instagram is a great way to create content that can benefit both your Instagram and Facebook page, so it is a good idea to learn how to create organic content for Instagram. You can create organic content on Instagram for three different locations: your newsfeed, story feed, or IGTV feed. Below, you will find information on how to create organic content for all three of these areas on Instagram, allowing you to gain the full benefit of Instagram and its many sharing features! You will also learn about hashtags, which are an essential tool for getting discovered by your target audience.

Newsfeed

Your newsfeed can be used for organic marketing by sharing images or one-minute video clips to your page. When you share on

Instagram, it is a good idea to ensure that all of your images carry a similar on-brand aesthetic so that your newsfeed develops in a way that is attractive and well put together. You do not want to be creating a feed that has too many different colors, subjects, or filters as this can create an aesthetic that is not visually appealing, thus minimizing your following. Instead, you may benefit from creating a vision board either through Instagram's saved images by saving images from your favorite followers and designing an aesthetic that way, or by creating a mood board on Pinterest. Once you have created your mood board, ensure that everything you share is relevant to that mood board and that you continue to develop that aesthetic through each new graphic and video. This will create a well-branded feed that attracts new followers to want to follow your page and pay attention—because it creates an attraction within them toward your brand.

Story Feed

Your story feed can be a little more flexible, as you do not necessarily need to keep all of your filters and colors the same on your story feed. While you do still want the subject and purpose of your stories to be clear and direct, having your story feed more flexible and open to free sharing is a great way to create a more personal connection with your audience. When your audience gets used to seeing your face and following your daily adventures in your story feed, they begin to feel like they are a part of your world. As a result, they develop a relationship with you that allows them to feel connected to you, which creates brand loyalty, and increases your chances of converting your audience into paying clients.

You can use your stories to share a live video as well, which can be a great opportunity for you to have even more personal interactions with your audience. In 2019, a big trend is sharing a live video stream with yourself and a friend who is in the same industry as you so that you can talk back and forth and enjoy shared live video. This can be a great opportunity for you to discuss information with your audience, share a more personal experience with your friend and your audience, and help your audience feel as though they are a part of your inner circle. On this live call, or if you choose to do one solo, you can simply talk about things relating to your industry that you feel will be interesting to your audience.

IGTV

Instagram television, or IGTV, is a platform that you can use to share even more with your audience. On IGTV you can share up to ten minutes of pre-recorded video with your audience in any way that you want to. This part of the platform operates similar to YouTube, except that videos are shot in portrait mode instead of landscape mode, so they are more accessible for mobile users.

Brands are using IGTV for many different things, from educational purposes to providing entertainment for their audiences. Some great examples include sharing tutorials, such as how to apply makeup or how to make a certain recipe, or informational videos, such as providing certain tips or knowledge to your audience through film. You can also go on IGTV to simply chat and share updates with your audience, such as a live vlog, as this can create a personal experience for your audience to enjoy, too.

Hashtags

Hashtags are a necessary part of the Instagram experience when it comes to growing your audience on Instagram. Hashtags are tools that people use to search for new content that interests them, and they are tools that posters use to get identified by the people searching for these very hashtags. You want to use hashtags on every picture you share, but you want to use them correctly to ensure that you are getting found by the right audience.

The easiest way to find new hashtags is to regularly search your industry on Instagram and see what similar and trending hashtags are arising to get an idea for what your audience is looking at consistently. This way, you can find all of the hashtags that are relevant to your industry and that can be used on your photographs.

You can use up to 30 hashtags per picture, so do not be afraid to go through and grab as many different hashtags as you want to on your pictures so that you can get found by as many people as possible. You can easily begin keeping potential hashtags in a list on your phone and then access them anytime you want to share new content with your audience so that you can choose relevant hashtags to use. Update your list regularly to ensure that you stay trending.

You can also use hashtags in your stories, although you should not use more than one or two per story to avoid being considered spam. Hashtags themselves can be followed on Instagram, and each one has a story feed with trending stories, so using hashtags gives you the potential to be found and watched by new potential followers. When you do use hashtags, make sure that you click the tag that comes up so that your story is actually associated with the hashtag. You will know it is complete when the hashtag is underlined, showing you that it has been linked to the hashtag feed.

Chapter 5: Twitter Marketing

Twitter is an incredibly powerful tool for influencer marketing, as well as many other marketing techniques. If you are already on Twitter, effectively branding your profile and learning how to leverage influencers on the platform is a wonderful way for you to begin growing into your next level of business. In this chapter, you are going to explore how you can leverage Twitter to grow your business, increase your audience, and reach the next phase of growth for you and your brand. If you are not already on Twitter, using this chapter can help you get started so that you can tap into this tool and grow your business on another great platform.

Branding Your Twitter Profile

Branding your Twitter profile effectively is an important way to make sure that you are creating a profile that is actually going to attract your target audience. When it comes to developing your Twitter reach, a well-developed profile is more clean and complete looking, meaning that people will stop and look at it longer, potentially even following you and engaging with your content. When you are developing your profile, it is important to create with your audience in mind so that they can get a feel for who you are and what you are creating. On Twitter, one study showed that more than

80 percent of people who land on your profile also check out your link, which means that this is a huge conversion you can be tapping into if you leverage your profile effectively.

There are six ways that you can brand your Twitter profile effectively so that your audience gets a complete experience when landing on your profile. These five branding tools are advanced, so whether you are new or mature on the platform, reading through these tips will help you leverage your platform and grow it even stronger.

Fill Out Your Entire Profile

With your brand in mind, make sure that you fill out your entire Twitter profile in a way that clearly reflects your brand. You can do this by ensuring that your username is on brand, your bio is filled out, and you have filled in your website information on your profile. You can also update your profile image with a properly sized branded image, header image, and background image. These three elements allow you to create a graphical aesthetic that is on-brand, making your account even more personalized and enjoyable. You should also place your city or town information in your profile so that people know where your business is located, even if you are a remote business so that you can give people an idea of where you are. Knowing where you are located helps people feel more confident that you are a real person with a location, and that you are not a scammer located overseas trying to get money from people. Essentially, it adds another layer to your online personality.

As you fill everything out, make sure that it all ties together and creates an appealing aesthetic so that your profile is visually enjoyable to spend time on. You want your profile to look attractive so that when people land on it, they are instantly curious to learn more because now you have created visual interest. You can even increase your visual interest by creating custom branding graphics for your page and switching them out every season, ensuring that your page keeps a fresh and attractive feel. Some brands will even adjust their header image every month or every other month as their specials change so that their header behaves like a promotional tool for their brand.

Follow the Right People

On Twitter, following the right people is an imperative tool in helping you generate engagement and get your name out there. When you follow the right people, you develop a group of people that you can engage with, so they begin to see who you are. As they do, they will start to follow you, giving you a following that is going to help you get started as these are the people who will start interacting with your posts as you begin posting them. Early on, really investing in the back and forth engagement process is important to help develop traction with your page, so make sure that you are spending a lot of time following people and then engaging with the people that you are following. As you do, be authentic with your sharing to ensure that you are not coming across as fake or like you are simply trying to use this engagement to grow. Even though that is part of the reason, there should also be the intention that you genuinely want to connect with these people and grow your platform.

Another way that you can use following people as a tool is through recognizing that by following the people in your industry, you are actually turning your feed into market research. When you are following all of the right people, such as people whom you look up to and people who are a part of your target audience, you get to see how your industry is growing and what is trending in your industry. This way, you can begin using the information to develop your content and keep yourself trending in your industry.

Tweet

Before you begin tweeting, there is one very important rule that needs to be made clear: *Twitter is not your electronic billboard.* Your goal when you get on Twitter is not to start blasting your wall with information and assuming that everyone is going to see what you have shared and begin interacting with you. No, Twitter is less about status updates and more about fostering interaction and engagement with your audience. You need to ensure that every update you make is not promoting your company, as this is going to come across as self-serving and spammy. Instead, make every fourth tweet promotional, and all of the others in between about engaging with your audience and starting conversations.

In addition to getting your ratios correct, you also want to make sure that what you are tweeting and how you are tweeting it is relevant to your audience. You want to use keywords that are relevant to your industry so that when people are searching these keywords, your tweets begin coming up. You should also be paying attention to trending keywords in your industry so that you can make use of these, thus increasing your chances of getting found on Twitter. Aside from that, make sure that you are using your personality and personal voice on Twitter so that people can tell you apart from the crowd. You will discover more about how you can use your personality on Twitter later in this very chapter!

Optimize for Mobile

Twitter is often used on a desktop, but it also has a widely popular mobile app, which means that you need to be thinking about your mobile users as well. In this day and age, there is nothing more frustrating than a business that breaks into the online space and refrains from developing any form of mobile optimization. It makes the business look incomplete and outdated since more and more people are switching to mobile devices as mobile browsers and applications continue to grow in popularity with each passing year.

Fortunately for you, the Twitter app is already optimized for mobile, so there is not much that you need to do to optimize your profile for the mobile app. The primary thing that you need to pay attention to is your graphics—since the graphics may appear differently on a mobile browser. Always take a look to ensure that you are not using an excessively tiny font or images with too intricate of details that are not as easily visible on mobile, as this can make it your profile frustrating to browse on mobile. Always make sure that anytime you update your images, you peek at what they look like on a mobile setting so that you are confident that what your audience is seeing is professional and easy to see.

Integrate Twitter Elsewhere

Lastly, a well-branded and well-established Twitter account should be integrated elsewhere beyond Twitter itself. Make sure to add follow buttons on your website, in your emails, and anywhere else that Twitter follow buttons can be added so that anytime someone comes across you online, they find your Twitter, too. If you run a blog, one particularly powerful integration is to use a plugin that allows you to feature relevant tweets in your blog posts so that people who are on Twitter can retweet your relevant tweets. This way, not only can they retweet you and get you in front of their audience, but they can also follow you and begin consuming even more of your content through Twitter, making it a win-win situation!

The Importance of Your Personality

When it comes to branding yourself anywhere online, making your personality clearly visible to the outside world is imperative. There is nothing worse than coming across a well-designed and well-positioned brand only to find that it lacks any true originality, making it sound just like every other brand that is attempting to grow in the online space. Getting your personality into your message and being authentic is an important part of really getting your message out there and growing as a personal brand.

This message applies not only for Twitter but for all personal branding strategies: if you are too afraid to speak up and be yourself, you are going to have a hard time getting heard by anyone who cares. The internet is filled with people who are afraid to be original because they are afraid to be rejected or disliked by the people around them. It can be scary to think about what might happen if you put yourself out there in a personal way and later find that you are not well received, on many levels. Even so, getting past this fear and putting yourself out there as far as your branding is concerned is necessary if you are going to get heard and develop yourself as a personal brand. You need to be willing to share your originality and show people the authentic side of you that makes you different from the crowd.

On Twitter specifically, do not be afraid to tweet with humor and share your real thoughts in relation to everything going on in the world. Talk about what you think, share your real opinions, and do not be afraid to be the real you. The more you share your authentic personality, the more people who are looking for someone just like you are going to find you and start paying attention to what you are saying. As a result, you will find yourself feeling a lot more received by your audience because they can actually find you.

As you continue sharing in this more authentic way, you will also begin to discover what types of conversations your audience enjoys having so that you know what to talk to them about. This way, you can start plenty of rich conversations through your posts, which goes a long way in terms of developing relationships with your audience. As people continue responding and developing these relationships with you, they will also continue to pay more attention to your sales posts, and will likely be more interested in paying attention to what it is that you are selling. Now, rather than just being another person promoting to them on Twitter, you are a genuine personality who is offering them a product or a service that they are interested in. You have taken the time to get to know them and develop a relationship with them, so now they trust when you say you have something that they may be interested in because they trust that you know them enough to know whether or not they actually would be.

As you can see, truly taking the time to invest in relationships online, especially on a social platform like Twitter, which thrives on conversation, you are doing your business and growth a massive favor. You want to continue emphasizing these conversations and relationships, and trust that through them, your business will grow massively and effectively.

Maximizing Growth

Once you get on Twitter, you must begin focusing on how you can maximize your growth quickly. The sooner you can develop a healthy following, the sooner you are going to be able to convert through Twitter as you will have a large enough audience to market to. Growing on Twitter is similar to growing on other platforms, although there are some strategies you can take into consideration to help you get your name out there more consistently, thus making it easier for people to find you. The thing that you need to remember about Twitter is that you need to make a big "splash" actually to get seen and followed by people. People follow those on Twitter who know how to be the life of the party, who can spark a conversation or jump in on a conversation and make it livelier, and who possess a high amount of charisma. If you want to excel on Twitter, you need to be prepared to become a loud expression of yourself so that you can be heard amongst the sea of other people who are also participating in conversations on Twitter. This is how you can go from being present to being present *and known.*

Because of how Twitter works—having a limited number of characters to use for updates and conversations—, you need to be ready to be upfront about what you are sharing from the get-go. In other words, do not waste your time burying the lead as this will result in you having your audience ignore you since they cannot get to the bottom of what you are trying to say. Be blunt, to the point, and very clear in what you are saying in every single post so that people always know what you are saying and what you mean.

Another thing you need to consider when it comes to growing on Twitter is that people are only going to see so many of the recent tweets on their pages—they are not on the platform all day every day scrolling to see what you and everyone else is saying. As a result, you can benefit from reiterating the same tweet in a few different ways to ensure that your entire audience sees what you have posted and gets the value out of the tweet that you have shared.

Make sure that you think before you tweet, as well. When it comes to thinking before you tweet, doing so can prevent you from sharing anything that may come across as derogatory or rude. For example, a company known as DiGiorno's pizza used a hashtag known for raising awareness around domestic violence to promote their pizza deals that week. They later had to issue a professional apology statement, as this came across as demeaning and rude to the people who were actually using the hashtag to promote something positive. Not all press is good press, especially in a generation of people who are becoming more and more consciously aware of how language and behaviors affect the people around them. Thinking critically about how your tweet will be received before making it is also especially important for smaller brands or personal brands who may not have as large of a following as existing corporations. For you, every follower counts, so you need to be mindful and respectful of your followers when you are generating posts.

Lastly, always give credit where credit is due as it does not come across as authentic or genuine to share someone else's content and appear as though you are attempting to pass it off as your own. Tagging the original content creator, using the acronym "RT" which stands for "retweet" or using the words "via" before sharing who originally shared the content can all help you give credit to the original content creator. Online, everyone is trying to make a living or get their name out there, so you have to be sure that you are being respectful to the other people who are also trying to generate success online. Furthermore, nothing will tank your success faster than making it appear as though you are attempting to take ownership of someone else's work. If you get caught plagiarizing content, you *will* be penalized for it, and likely very harshly. A great example of this is Audrey Kitching, who has a massive online following, and an equally massive number of people resisting her because they have found that she regularly steals content. Whether or not she actually does is unimportant; the fact is that she has become well known for this behavior and, as a result, has stunted her growth in a big way. If you stay authentic and always give credit where credit is due, then you can keep your reputation clean and your audience happy. Integrity is key.

Finding Influencers on Twitter

Twitter is another great platform for discovering influencers on, and leveraging influencers on Twitter is an equally excellent way to get your brand out there even further. Finding influencers on Twitter is similar to finding them elsewhere—you begin searching for content that is relevant to your industry, and then you start searching for the individuals who are making the biggest impact on Twitter through their posts. The key here is to know what you are looking for so that as you vet your Twitter influencers, you can be confident that you are getting the best ones. Unlike on Instagram or Facebook, vetting Twitter influencers is done in a slightly different way.

When you are looking for an influencer on Twitter, start by getting clear on the type of influencer that you are looking for. Ideally, you should be writing down what it is that they share, how they connect with your target audience, and what their personality is like. You want to find influencers who are sharing content that is relevant to what you offer, who connect with your target audience in a way that makes them likely to make sales, and who has a personality that will be a positive reflection for your brand. Finding the right influencer who is going to compliment your brand effectively is important to ensure that any money you invest into this influencer deal is going to be well spent, and you are going to get positive gains out of it.

Once you have identified who it is that you are looking for, you can begin finding influencers in your field who match these characteristics. Make sure that you are looking for people who fit these three categories first, as these need to be your priorities in whom you are searching for. You can pay attention to follower count and engagement content after—when you have identified a few people who already fit your needs as a brand.

When you are ready to begin looking at the influencer's metrics, you want to pay attention to engagement ratio more than anything else. On Twitter, a large following does not necessarily equal a large impact, so you need to be careful to ensure that the person you intend to work with does actually receive a high engagement ratio. The better their engagement ratio, the higher your chances of getting conversions through that influencer. Of course, this does come with a certain condition. If you have found someone who has incredible engagement ratios yet they are only getting engagement from tens of people or maybe a few hundred people, you are likely looking at someone who is not going to be able to create the impact that you need or desire. You want someone who has a high engagement ratio that earns them several hundred or even several thousand engagements per post, to ensure that they are someone who will make an impact. Once you have secured that fact, you can begin making content with your potential influencers so that you can start making deals with them. At this point, everything you do is going to be the same as you would have done on any other social media platform. You will still want to conduct yourself professionally, create legal documents outlining your deals, and be cooperative so that the influencer enjoys working with you and is likely to boost your reputation rather than minimize it due to your own misrepresentation of your brand.

Increasing the Value of Influencers

Increasing the value of influencers in terms of how they benefit your business comes in two ways: ensuring that you enter the right deals, and ensuring that you have the right perception of the partnership so that you can get the most out of it. Many businesses will enter a partnership with an influencer, believing that they are doing what is best for their business, only to later discover that their lack of research or their rigid agreements results in them not gaining much out of their influencers at all. To help you increase the value that you gain from your influencers, start with first things first: you need to make sure that you are finding the right influencers who are targeting your convertible market audience and are getting a high enough engagement ratio. If you are getting into agreements with people who are not reaching your true audience or making a big enough impact with their strategies, you will struggle to make any conversions at all. As a result, anything you have invested into influencers may be considered a waste because you have spent too much time with the wrong people who were unable to generate the results that you were seeking.

Once you find the right people who can generate the best results for you, the next step is to make sure that you check yourself and have the right expectations for how the partnership is going to look. If you are working with the right people, it is important to know that they are influencers as a part of their career, so they know what they are doing. They know how to reach out to people, make an impact, and get seen, which is exactly why you hired them in the first place. Attempting to set too many rules or restrictions around how they are to complete work for you is only going to result in you feeling as though nothing is being accomplished because you have limited their creative expression. Assuming you have hired correctly, the person you have hired knows exactly how to craft posts so that they get seen, so that people interact with them, and so that conversions happen. For that reason, you need to trust the influencer to do their job and respect that they are going to know what is needed more so than you are.

It is imperative that even if you are a professional marketer or you have a certain way you like things done that you still give your influencer creative direction rights. While you are absolutely entitled to give an idea for what you want it to look and sound like and the results you want to have, the rest should remain up to the influencer. They know how to sound authentic and share with their specific audience in a memorable way, so trust them.

Next, you need to make sure that you are clear on what it is that you should be doing to support the influencer in reviewing and promoting your products or services. Know what needs to be sent to them or offered to them, what type of support they need, and what timeline they need to work with to make the biggest impact with you. Make sure that you work your budget around being able to afford these things, as these are people who will truly help you, so in the long run, it is certainly worth it.

Lastly, once the influencer has done their part of sharing your products and services, do not be afraid to retweet their posts to your page, or even share their tweets to other platforms so that you can increase the reach. Having your brand name associated with certain well-known influencers in your industry can be massive, even on other platforms, so do not be afraid to co-create this process with the influencer and really get the word out there. Ideally, you should allow them to share to Twitter first, and then you can share their tweet out to other platforms over the next couple of days so that the impact carries on for as long as possible. If that person is on another platform as well, make sure that you continue tagging them in each post that you share so that they gain credit for crafting the post itself. This will also get you seen by their audience on other platforms, which extends your reach even further, allowing you to really gain maximum value from your deal with the influencer.

Tracking Your Metrics

The final part about really making a splash on Twitter is learning how to track your metrics so that you can get yourself in front of your audience and continue growing in front of them. Knowing how to track your metrics, or your analytics as some people call them, allows you to discover where you are making the biggest impact online and where you need to be doing better. When you discover where you are making the biggest impact, you can use this information to continue generating similar content and making an even bigger impact. When you discover areas where you are not performing so well, you can avoid recreating any content like that so that you are not continuing to create content that people do not care about.

Tracking your metrics on Twitter is simple. To track them, you need to have a business account, which you can convert to from the settings page of your account. If you do not yet have a business account, you will need to convert and then give your account time to build up metrics as Twitter will not check back through previous posts to see what your metrics are—it will only start tracking once you convert. Typically, you will want to give your account two to four weeks to really generate plenty of organic analytic metrics so that you can get a clear feel for how well your content is performing. If you attempt to start tracking too quickly, you might find that you do not see the full picture as you have not had enough types of content live out full lifespans on Twitter to really know.

After your analytics have been growing for a while, you can go ahead and open up your Tweet activity dashboard. Right from this dashboard, you will see information such as how many people have seen your content, how many times you have been retweeted, and how many likes and replies you have received from each tweet you have shared. These metrics are going to show you what content you are sharing that is being well received by your audience. As you look at these metrics, you can begin noticing what trends rise through the content that your audience likes most so that you have a clear idea of what you can begin sharing more of for your audience. For example, you may find that your humor or satire related content gains higher views than your serious content. In this case, you can begin using humor or satire to communicate with your audience in a better way, and you can even weave this tone of voice into your marketing content so that you can begin receiving more traction on your marketing content.

The next thing you want to pay attention to is your audience insights, as this information will tell you how much your audience has grown by and what demographic(s) your audience belongs to. This is important to pay attention to as, obviously, you want to receive consistent growth from your audience to ensure that you are heading in the right direction and increasing your impact online. You also want to make sure that you are paying attention to the demographic of who your audience is, as growth in a demographic that is extremely irrelevant to your industry is not necessarily a good thing. Although these are followers, they are not necessarily leads or people who are going to potentially buy from you, which means that although you are receiving high numbers of followers and engagement, you are still not likely going to be able to convert that audience. You want to have an audience that is going to resonate with what you have to offer to ensure that you will convert them at some point.

If you find that your demographic is vastly different from the one that you need to be reaching, you need to start doing more research around what your target audience is doing on Twitter. Pay attention to where they are hanging out, what they are talking about, and what makes them engage with a brand. Then, you can begin paying attention to how your brand is different from what they are already following, and how you can begin leveraging that information to make the necessary adjustments in your brand and your approach to help you reach your ideal audience. Sometimes, especially early on, it can take many minor adjustments as you learn to connect with your audience and have an impact on engaging with them and sparking their interest. Soon enough, you will find that proper balance and sharing with your audience will be effortless! Use your metrics to help you identify where your strengths and weaknesses are to minimize the amount of time that it will take to get your brand out there and really grow at a substantial rate.

Chapter 6: YouTube and Podcasts

Currently, in 2019, audio and visual marketing are two of the most powerful tools that you can use to get in front of your audience since these are the two styles of content that audiences are consuming the most. These days, throwing on a podcast or a YouTube video while you cook dinner, drive to work, or hit the gym is part of how the modern adult gets their content. Rather than having to sit and scroll a wall for countless hours or read something, they can multi-task, which allows personal development, education, or entertainment to overlap other important tasks. This method of consuming content is perfect for the busy lifestyle that everyone seems to subscribe to with their careers, families, social lives, and personal lives.

If you really want to skyrocket your personal brand, having either a YouTube channel, a podcast, or both is a great opportunity to get your content in front of your audience. This way, they have another excellent way to consume your content, you can share even more, and you are establishing a more personal connection through either voice or voice and visual. As your audience gets used to hearing your voice and, if you have a YouTube channel, seeing your face, they will grow even more attached to you and your brand. This way, they begin to feel like they are truly your friends and want to connect more frequently. As a brand, this means that you can offer even more products and services, and they will genuinely want more from you as they enjoy gaining the value that you have to offer.

The Power of Audio and Visual Marketing

Audio and visual marketing has always been powerful—that is why radio and television have both succeeded, and why so many commercials exist on radio and television. Understand that these two methods of marketing have been used for generations because they work, and they work because they have been used for generations. In the past, audio and visual marketing really took off because they were similar to word of mouth marketing, except that they could be done widespread. Because it has been done for so long, people have also grown used to developing "relationships" of sorts with others heard on the radio or television. In modern times, radio and television are still relevant, but audio and visual marketing through the internet have grown to become widely popular as well. Not surprisingly, the growth of these two areas of popularity has also led to most platforms offering some form of audio or visual marketing services that you can take advantage of when you are marketing online! For example, Instagram and Facebook have live video marketing features, and Twitter offers the opportunity to upload your video content to be shared with your audience.

If you really want to make audio or visual content your primary method of interaction, however, relying on these apps that only incorporate audio and visual marketing as a small segment of the overall picture is not ideal. Instead, you should seek to use a platform that nurtures audio or visual marketing specifically, such as a podcast platform or YouTube. This way, you can specialize in offering audio or visual content, and your audience can consume plenty of it through your sharing. You can also continue to grow your other platforms so that you can promote your podcast or YouTube across other platforms, increasing your viewer reach and growing your shows more rapidly. You will learn more about this later.

In the meantime, understand that people are wired to trust word of mouth as being one of the most reliable tools when it comes to receiving advice on where to buy things, and what to buy. When you tap into using audio and visual content for marketing, and especially when you are using both together, you are offering your audience a very powerful tool to see you, hear you, and trust you. Most people are far more likely to trust and act on what they have heard through spoken content over what they have read on yet another status update. This does not mean that written content marketing and status updates do not work—just that they may not be as effective in a marketplace where many people are already sharing plenty of written content marketing. Moreover, written marketing lacks the auditory and visual aids that podcasts and video content offer.

YouTube, Podcast, or Both?

You may be wondering what type of content is going to be the best for you to develop, and the truth is: only you are going to have the right answer. Part of what you decide is going to be based on how your audience would rather consume content, and the other part is based on what type of content you are interested in creating. Below, you will find what to consider to help you decide whether you want to do YouTube videos, podcasts, or both.

If you are considering YouTube videos, the chances are that you are intrigued by the idea of offering video content to your audience. Video content is great for a brand who wants to share visual aids or representations, such as drawings on a whiteboard or physical product demonstrations, or who simply wants to have their face recognizable by their audience. Using video content can help you convey your attitude and emotions through facial expressions, which, for some people, makes a big difference. YouTube also operates as a social media style site, making it easy to upload videos and promote them to your audience, as you can upload a video on

YouTube and then share that video to other platforms. Some common drawbacks of YouTube include that you need to be able to film in 1080p or higher with high-quality lighting conditions and visual aesthetics in general, and your audience cannot download your videos, so they cannot always take you on the go.

Podcasts are great for taking on the go as they can be downloaded and listened to whenever. That being said, for you, uploading your show to several different platforms can be challenging, although necessary, if you want to get your show out there in front of a wide audience. You also want to make sure that you are creating a high sound quality, as your audience is going to want to hear high-quality sound coming from your show. Aside from that, podcasts are excellent because they are very easy for people to consume, and the apps for listening to podcasts are often convenient and easy to navigate for you and your audience. And, when you are uploading a podcast, you do not have to worry about what you look like or what the quality of the aesthetics are in your environment as you can simply sit somewhere quiet and speak.

Generally speaking, if you want to maximize your outreach and increase your potential of serving your audience, doing both a podcast and a YouTube show at the same time can be valuable. This does require more leg work on your end, but it is not too challenging, so you can certainly make it work if you want to maximize your outreach. Overall, the only steps that would be added would be: splitting your audio from your visual for your podcast and then doing the groundwork and promotion for both of them. In many cases, you can promote both at the same time as a "listen or watch, based on your preference" type of marketing strategy. Although this may sound challenging, it can all be done with iMovie or an equivalent program, and then by following the steps to upload and promote both a podcast and a YouTube channel. If you can endure the added steps, this may be the best opportunity for you to maximize your outreach and hit your fullest potential online.

Designing Your "Show"

Once you have decided on how you are going to present your show, you also want to do the groundwork to design your show. When it comes to designing shows, you want to make sure that you have a very clear focus that you take with your show. If your brand does not entirely revolve around the show itself, you may wish to choose one singular aspect of your brand to turn into a show and grow the rest elsewhere. The clearer your show's focus is, the better you will market it and get the right audience listening. When it comes to videos or audio, people want to have a very clear reason to listen to ensure that they are getting everything they need or want from the show. If your direction is unclear, people may not listen to your show as they may not be interested in spending twenty to 40 minutes trying to find out what direction you are going with it.

A great example of picking a clear focus with your show would be one revolving around marketing. Say you are a marketing agency which helps people market their small businesses so that they can make a larger impact in reaching their audience. Perhaps the service you offer is marketing consultations and done-for-you marketing packages, but you want to create a bigger reach, so you want to offer something that is free value right away. If this were the case, you might launch a show that would be geared toward teaching people how to take advantage of the latest social media marketing trends so that they can begin to give it a try themselves. You could also market your done-for-you marketing packages or consultations throughout your show so that people who were interested in understanding the trends but who felt they might need help enforcing them could hire you. This is a great way to leverage your show as a tool to position you as the expert in your field, as well as to use it for a marketing tool, and to increase your audience by offering free value that they can begin utilizing right away.

Once you have decided on the focus of your show, you also need to decide on the details of your show. Figure out what you want the show to be named, how long you want each episode to be, and how frequently you want to be uploading your episodes. You can also come up with a structure for how you will be naming your episodes, if you desire, so every episode is named similarly, allowing your audience to grow used to your podcast or YouTube channel's brand. Ideally, you should be creating shows that are ten to 60 minutes in length, and uploading them at least once per week to develop a frequency that is consistent enough to reach your audience and keep them returning for more. You should upload your videos or podcasts on the same day every week so that people know when they can expect to receive more from you.

Leveraging YouTube for Brand Recognition

YouTube is a powerful platform for anyone who wants to develop brand recognition. When you get on YouTube, you can give your audience a visual about who you are, what you are like, and what you have to offer. YouTube is an excellent platform because it is hosted like a search engine site, which means that people can discover you organically even after your videos have been uploaded—sometimes even years later. Moreover, since the videos are always easy to locate on your channel, people can binge-watch your content, or you can go back and share old (but still relevant) content at a later date with your audience. In this way, your YouTube content will get you much further than nearly any other form of content out there because its lifespan is so long.

YouTube should be leveraged by either bringing your audience into your personal world or by teaching them something, as these are the two things that people watch most on YouTube. If you want to bring people into your world, you can try vlogging as a way to create a personal relationship with your audience. Vlogging is done by bringing your audience with you throughout the day, or the week, and showing them parts of your life that you think they will resonate most with. Some vloggers will show absolutely everything, whereas others may show their daily routines that are relevant to their brand.

Decide what you feel most comfortable with sharing and what your audience is going to be most interested in and start by sharing that, as everything else will be discovered later on.

If you would rather share how-to videos, make sure that you choose an area within your industry that a lot of information can be shared on. Additionally, to help you to continue having more content to talk about, make each video very direct and about just one thing. Refrain from giving too much at once, or you may find that you run out of things to offer and talk about. Remember to plan long term so that you can keep your channel going and growing for a significant period, as a well-designed YouTube channel can be a powerful source of growth for many brands.

Once you have developed your YouTube channel and begun uploading pages to it, leverage it by sharing it everywhere. Show people that you have been making videos, give them a small idea of what to expect, and drive them over to your channel. You can also embed your video on your website or in email newsletters so that people can begin watching it directly on your site or in your emails. The more you put it out there, the more your page is going to be viewable by your audience, and as people grow to see you as having the page that is sharing the best and most relevant content to your industry, they will want to keep watching you.

Maximizing Your YouTube Growth Potential

As with anything, your biggest growth potential is to tap into consistency, as the more consistent you are, the more people are going to believe in you and what you have to offer. Consistency will help you, especially when it comes to showing your audience that you are serious, and reminding them that you have plenty of content available for them to watch. Sometimes, you are going to come across peoples' feeds at a time where they cannot commit to watching, but you might find that you can be watched at a later date. If you were to stop sharing your channel, they might simply forget about you, but because you are continuously sharing your content, these people remember that your channel exists and will watch whenever they can.

Another thing you want to do to maximize your growth on YouTube is to design your channel. Go through and create your YouTube channel name, upload a profile picture, upload channel art, and use attractive thumbnails for your videos so that people see your thumbnails and are more inspired to watch your videos. You can also create a custom channel trailer so that when people land on your channel, they can learn a few facts about you, what you have to offer, and why they should be watching your channel.

As well, make sure that you are taking advantage of SEO strategies. SEO is a powerful tool that you can use to get your videos higher in YouTube rankings, as the more you fill out for SEO, the more your videos are going to rank. The best way to optimize your channel for YouTube is to ensure that you are always filling out the tags on your videos, using descriptions that are rich with keywords, and choosing titles with relevant keywords. You can discover what keywords are trending around your particular video topic by going to a website like Google Keywords and searching for relevant keywords. This way, your video has plenty of information filled out in it that allows YouTube to realize that it is relevant to someone's search terms, thus allowing it to rank higher. The more views and shares you get, the more relevant your video looks; therefore, the higher you rank once again, so do not be afraid to encourage people to view your video, comment on it, subscribe to your page, and share the video with their friends.

Leveraging Your Podcast for Brand Recognition

Leveraging your podcast for brand recognition will operate similarly to YouTube, except that you cannot physically show things to people so you will need to refrain from attempting to teach anything that may require visual aid. Instead, you want to rely more on talking and audio-based learnings that do not require your audience actually to see anything that you are doing. A great example would be discussing strategies for increasing your visibility on Instagram or talking people through the process of healing from a breakup. Offering people educational, entertainment-based, or informational content through voice clips is a great opportunity to get yourself out there without having to show anything to your audience physically.

One great way to leverage your podcast is to center your podcast around weekly themes and then talk about those themes on other social media platforms throughout the week, too. This way, you can allow your content to all come together to offer a central lesson and support your audience in growing. This also helps market your podcast, as you can talk about the same topic all week and let people know that a podcast is coming out with even more information, and then drop the podcast. This marketing strategy will pull your audience in and keep them paying attention so that when your podcast launches, people will quickly pay attention to it and, hopefully, share it with those whom they think will benefit from it, too.

You can also leverage your podcast by using marketing strategies throughout the entire podcast. For example, you could say something like: "This next tip I'm going to give you is actually one I gave my client last week, and I realized it really needs to be shared more widely. Of course, we had an hour to talk about it so I could go much more in-depth, but I'm going to give you the gist of it right now so that you can begin benefitting from it, too." This is a great way to begin marketing yourself by showing people that those who work with you get way more, but you also want them to benefit right now. This way, those who begin implementing your strategies will see that they work and may choose to work with you at a later date because they realize that your strategies really do get them benefits. Alternatively, if they want all of the value you have to offer, they may wish to begin working with you right away so that they do not have to attempt to implement it themselves or only get part of the benefits when they want to gain the full benefits.

Maximizing Your Podcast Growth Potential

Maximizing your growth on your podcast will work similarly to YouTube in that you want to remain consistent and talk about it as often as possible. The more you are talking about your podcast and sharing it with people, the more people are going to find you and start listening to your podcast, or listening to it at a later date if they have forgotten to tune in one week. Over time, people will grow attached to your podcast and will want to watch it consistently because they enjoy hearing from you and connecting with your content.

Another great way to grow your podcast is through networking, as the more you network with people, the more people you will have to tell about your podcast. You can talk about your podcast with every organic opportunity you gain as a way to get your name out there, let people know what you are doing, and give them a chance to listen to the content that you have produced. While you do not want to go overboard talking about it, as no one likes obsessive unsolicited marketing, you do want to make sure that you share as much as you can with your audience. The more you can talk about it, the better.

Another great tool to help you maximize your growth is to pick a good host right from the start. Nothing would be more frustrating than starting out with a low tier host and having to switch everything over at a later date, so do your best to avoid this at all costs by starting out with a high-quality host. You want to look for a host that is reasonably priced, will put your show out to every single podcast platform like RSS, Apple Podcasts, and iTunes, and will allow you to continue to grow as long as your network grows. You can always start with a free or basic account on a great platform, but do your best to think like a pro and get into a pro account as soon as possible, as this is the best way to ensure that you are really getting yourself out there and growing quickly.

If you are going to be using a YouTube page and podcast, be sure to cross-promote whenever possible. If you have shared the same show as a video and a podcast, each time you upload content to your platform, make sure that you market both kinds with posts that say something like "Watch here, or listen here!" with links to your respective shows. The more you can cross-promote, the more options your viewers have to watch or listen to you, and the more likely you are going to maximize your podcast and YouTube growth substantially.

Chapter 7: Blogging and Bloggers

For years now, people have been talking as though the blogging world is dying and there is no real point to get into blogging anymore as the world is "saturated" and "no one is reading blogs anymore." To be honest, this "the industry is dead" talk happens in nearly every industry every year, and the only people who believe it are the people who are unwilling to educate themselves on how they can leverage that industry effectively. Contrary to this message, blogging continues to be a highly effective way to get content out to your audience, generate evergreen content that can be viewed at any time, and push your website up search engine rankings by adding more keywords to your website. Getting your blog out there is a great opportunity to show everyone your expertise while also expanding your brand and growing your presence, so there is absolutely no reason for you to stop or avoid blogging in 2019.

If you are already blogging, you may be wanting to grow your platform even larger so that you can have greater success. If you are new to blogging, you may be wondering how you can leverage your blog to grow your presence so that the rest of your brand receives a positive boost from your brand, helping you to grow even larger online. In this chapter, you will discover how to grow your blog, how to use your blog to grow your brand, and what you can do to leverage blogging influencers in 2019 so that you can have a massive impact. This is everything you need to use to get started, grow larger, and dominate the blogosphere.

Growing Your Branded Blog

The first step in growing your branded blog is making sure that your blog is well branded and attractive. If you have been blogging for a while, the chances are that you have been steadily putting in the work to brand your blog and keep it attractive for your audience, but if you are "brand-new", you may not have done this part yet. The best way to brand your blog is to look at your brand elsewhere online and begin branding it accordingly so that your blog matches the brand that you have already begun to develop. You can also begin branding and marketing your blog by talking about it on social media and giving people the information they need to get excited about the fact that you have a blog coming out very soon!

As you grow your branded blog, you must continue to grow it with an authentic voice. Sometimes, when people step into a new world of marketing or sharing, they feel as though they need to adjust their voice to match the audience that is most likely to meet them on the platform. This may be an attempt to serve your audience, or it may be because you simply do not know how to expand your voice into a blog, but either way attempting to change your voice or your perspective to fit your blog is going to take away from the greatness of your blog. People have grown to know you for how you speak, what your perspectives are, and what you have to offer, and they are going to want to continue to gain information from you with that same personality. Otherwise, people may begin to think that your personality is inauthentic, or that your blog is not enjoyable and therefore they may never actually pay any attention to it, which can lead to a lot of wasted time.

If you are unaware of how to expand your brand into a blog, review your brand's personality and pay attention to what the likely dialogue between your brand and its audience would be in a more long-form method like blogging. The more you can identify what your key personalities are and what your sound is, the easier it is going to be for you to start generating content for your blog in a way that sounds authentic. If you still do not know, a great way to start blogging is to voice record yourself speaking what you want your blog post to be about so that it sounds authentic and how you would speak. Then, you can simply transcribe what you have said and edit it so that it looks polished for a blog post. This is a great way to keep your voice sounding authentic and personal when you are blogging so that people can still feel your personality in everything that you share.

Lastly, make sure that you pay attention to the technical aspects of your blog when it comes to planning for growth as well. You can do this by ensuring that you have a search box, clear navigation menu, and easy to understand layout for your blog so that people can easily find what they are looking for. You should also make your blog mobile friendly to ensure that all of your mobile users know that they can visit your page and still gain value from it, rather than having to struggle with strange text sizes and weird content layouts on their mobile screens. Thinking in this more technical way ensures that you develop a blog that is approachable and useable by your audience so that they can actually enjoy your blog. Every time you make a change on your blog, make sure that you take a look at it from a reader's point of view on both your desktop and mobile browser to confirm that you have made it readable by your audience. This way, you avoid losing readers solely based off of minor technical discrepancies.

The World of Blogging Influencers

Back before social media really blew up, YouTube and blogging were two of the most widely used platforms for influencers. At one time, social media was exclusively used by influencers to drive their audiences back to their YouTube pages or blogs so that they could market to their audiences in a space where they could offer more information. For this reason, blogging became a huge platform for influencers to exist on so that they could make a great income from their audience and the brands that wanted access to their audience. These days, blogging is still a massive platform for influencers to use so that they can continue getting out there in front of their audience. Although not every single one of their audience members is going to click back to their blog, there is still a massive majority of people who would prefer to look at a full blog post and get the entire scoop on a new product or service before they actually buy it. By having a blog available, influencers can continue to offer this greater amount of information to their audience so that they can give their audience plenty of content to read.

These days, how blogging influencers work is slightly different. Rather than requiring everyone to go to their blog for information on how to purchase something, they offer the information right away on social media posts and then offer more information on their blog for anyone who prefers to receive more information before purchasing. This way, they can target the audience members who are not interested in learning as much, as well as the ones who feel that they need to read more to have a more well-rounded decision before purchasing products.

Either way, almost every true influencer will have a blog or website of sorts to show businesses and followers that they are truly running an influencer business. This is also a great way for them to create a deeper personality showcase for their audience so that everyone can get a better feel for who they are and what they have to offer.

In 2019, connecting with blogging influencers is mostly driven by getting on Google or a similar search engine and searching for popular bloggers in your industry. This is the easiest way to find influencers who are also taking advantage of blogging so that you can collaborate with them through the blogosphere. The reason why you want to have influencers who are on blogs specifically is because these are individuals who will collaborate with you in a way that drives more traffic to your blog. You can certainly collaborate on your personal blog with those who do not have a blog, though it is hard to determine whether or not their audience is interested in reading blogs, as not all audiences are.

Once you have identified influencers in the blogosphere through a search engine, you can begin following them and consuming their content to get a feel for who they are. You can also take a look to see where else they are online and how their engagement out in social media is—to get a better feel for the quality of the influence that this particular blogger has and whether or not they can help you get the publicity that you seek. Should you find that they match your ideals for a collaboration, you can always get into contact with them to "put the feelers out". Often, bloggers who are open to collaborate will have some easy form of contact that will let you know how to get in touch with them. If they do not, email them at the link provided and follow the steps for getting in touch with influencers from Chapter 3, where you are introduced to the steps for ethically contacting influencers and creating collaboration deals with them.

Leveraging Collaborations

In the blogging world, collaborations are a powerful way to work together with other bloggers to provide greater value to your audience while also cross-promoting and receiving a greater reach to a new audience. Collaborations are often done as a way to provide new and unique content to an audience while still offering something that is on-brand or relevant to what the audience is typically interested in. There are two types of collaborations: writing on someone else's blog (outgoing collaborations,) or someone else writing on your blog (incoming collaborations.) Most often, collaborations will exist in both directions, as you write something for their audience and they write something for yours. Below, you will discover what it takes to be a part of either style of collaboration.

Outgoing Collaborations

When you want to write on someone else's blog, this is considered to be an outgoing collaboration as you are posting on someone else's page. Outgoing collaborations are a little harder to create as it is typically not considered ethical to ask someone else to host you on their blog. Instead, it is more common to request someone else to be hosted on your blog for a day, and then if they desire to, they can offer the same opportunity back to you. The one time where it may be more reasonable to offer an outgoing collaboration is if you know the blogger that you want to offer the outgoing collaboration to as a friend, and often, you will offer it as an exchanged collaboration where you both post for each other. This way, you are not simply asking to be hosted on a blog belonging to someone that you do not know that well.

If you do get offered to be a part of an outgoing collaboration, you need to make sure that you are cooperative and friendly to ensure that the collaboration goes well. If you are not, the other person may change their mind, and you might end up having your reputation muddied online, which can make it harder for you to grow through collaborations or even organically if the word gets out about your reputation. The best way to ensure that you remain cooperative and friendly is to keep the terms of the agreement very clear and ensure that both you and the person hosting the blog are both clear on what needs to be done. Stay clear on what you are posting about, when you will have the post submitted by, and what type of marketing you will do for the post that is being hosted on someone else's blog. Remaining open and clear about these things ensures that your lines of communication are never crossed, that everyone knows what to expect, and that if anything goes wrong, you can continue to communicate your way through it. Refrain from entering deals that are not clear, or at least not before clarifying them, as doing so can result in you coming off as uncooperative simply because you did not fully understand what was expected. It is better to be overcautious than under cautious, but do not feel the need to be cautious to the point of skepticism. Simply remain mindful of the agreement and keep your agreement clear so that you can both enjoy the process of working together.

Incoming Collaborations

If you want to host someone on your blog, make sure that you follow the steps of ethically connecting with influencers or other bloggers in Chapter 3 so that you come across as positive and friendly when you connect with potential collaborations. Then, when you have someone who agrees to collaborate with you, ensure that you continue to handle the collaboration professionally and ethically the entire way. It can be easy to want to become buddies with other bloggers, and while being friendly and even friends is certainly a good idea, it is always important to confirm that you are both clear on the fact that your blogs are your brands and that you want your brands to be respected by the other blogger. Staying friendly but professional during every exchange, keeping your expectations clear and reasonable, and working together with the person who will be posting on your blog is important. This is the best way to guarantee that you are collaborating in a way that is positive for both you and the person writing on your blog.

It is central that when you do this type of collaboration, you have the other blogger send you their blog post in a document and not give them the information to log into your blog to post. Remember: even if this is a professional transaction, you do not know this person, so you do not want them to have free access to your website and personal information. Stay friendly but smart. Moreover, ensure that they know exactly what type of content you are looking for so that when they submit their document to you, they are submitting content that is relevant to your audience and what you are looking for. It would be unfair to request someone to post on your page only to have them need to rewrite their post for you because you were unclear about what you wanted for your page. Remember: their time is valuable too, so respect it.

Lastly, when doing incoming collaborations, always make sure that you look for quality and not quantity. Ideally, you do not want too many incoming collaborations anyway as it will dilute the amount of content you have personally created for your website, which can leave your blog looking inauthentic. You want your audience to be very clear about who owns the blog. It can also make it look like the only purpose of your blog is to gain attention since you are constantly hosting everyone else on it. Furthermore, having low-quality bloggers on your page can be underwhelming and leave the quality of your blog going downhill. Treat your blog like your business and be intentional about who posts on it and what they are posting so that the quality of your blog stays high.

Growing Your Readership

There are many powerful ways for you to grow your readership on your blog, and learning how to do so effectively is necessary if you want to grow your blog massively. You have likely already covered the basics of sharing your blog posts to your social media platforms, so you are now going to extend beyond that when it comes to sharing your blog with others. In this section, you are going to explore some more advanced ways that you can begin developing your blog and growing your readership so that you can make a bigger impact with your blog in 2019.

The first thing that you need to do to grow your blog is to network with other bloggers, which can easily be done by joining Facebook groups or community forums where bloggers come together to support each other with growth. Connecting with bloggers in this way gives you a great opportunity to start networking with people, and this network can provide you with a great deal of growth opportunities if you continue to nurture it. When you connect with other bloggers, you can gain support from these bloggers in many ways, ranging from having them inspire you to try new techniques with your blogging or marketing, to having them recommend you to their readers or followers for content like yours. The key here is to make sure that you are contributing to your network, too, as people will not want to support you and offer you growth opportunities if you are not offering the same back. Be sure to be generous in recommending the bloggers from your network and creating opportunities for your network to grow as well by also bringing new inspiration and information into the community. The more you support others in a genuine and meaningful way, the more others are going to want to support you, which means that you all can grow your blogs much larger.

Another thing you can do to start growing your readership is contributing to top blogs in your niche so that your name gets out there and people can find you. For example, if you are a business blogger, you may consider contributing to *Forbes* so that *Forbes'* audience can discover you and, as a result, people can locate your blog as well. Other great examples of blogs like this include *Psychology Today*, *The Disney Blog*, *Babble*, and any other blog that is well known for serving a certain niche with a variety of different user-generated content posts. Note that contributing to these blogs is done differently depending on what blog you are looking into, so you are going to need to find their contributor's page and discover what steps are required for you to contribute to the blog itself.

The next piece of advice may be obvious, but it is worth noting: make sure that you are always posting content that your audience actually wants to be reading. Nothing is worse than posting and having no one read, so if this is happening, you need to seriously consider the fact that you may be posting content that your audience is not reading because it is not interesting to them—that or they have already heard it elsewhere multiple times, and they are tired of hearing the same content reiterated by every blogger there is. Make sure that you are making relevant and fresh content that your audience wants to read and can gain value from so that you can attract them to your page. If until now you have been writing based on what interested you most and not necessarily researching what your readers what to be consuming, now is the time to learn how to identify what your audience cares about so that you can begin making content that is relevant to them. You can do this by first doing a keyword search to see what keywords are currently trending in your industry, as these will give you an idea of what areas you should be focusing on when it comes to writing new content.

Once you have identified what keywords are trending, you need to determine what the right topic will be, and what angle you need to take on that topic to reach your audience effectively. You can do this by looking back at what type of content has already been working for you to see what your audience likes most, and by seeing what is working best for your competition as well. Realize that you do not want to directly copy your competition as this will only result in you having regurgitated content on your page, but getting an idea for how they are succeeding can help you with getting inspiration for how you want to display your content to the world.

Next, start seeing where your audience hangs out online and begin paying attention to the conversations that they are having and what their opinions and curiosities are. When you get a feel for what conversations your audience is having, it allows you to start deciding what your opinion is and how your opinion may be seen as beneficial or interesting to your audience. This way, you can start talking about what is relevant to your audience and in a way that is going to help them begin understanding more about the topic—thus making your blog interesting, informative, or both.

Next, start tracking the metrics of your blog so that you can get a feel for what your audience is enjoying the most. When you get an understanding of what content your audience likes the most, it becomes easier for you to begin offering this content more consistently so that your audience can continue coming back for more of what they like. Pay attention to how many people are viewing your posts and what type of additional engagement they are getting so that you can grow your page even larger. If you find that there is a trend in the content that your audience is not a big fan of, make a note of that as well and be sure to reduce the amount of content you share that revolves around that trend to avoid wasting time producing content that people are not particularly fond of.

Lastly, you want to grow your blog even larger by making promotion a part of your blog strategy. Rather than making your strategy simple and just posting and then sharing to social media sites, make an actual strategy that you are going to follow to get your blog out there and grow even larger. Pay attention to strategies that allow you to promote what you are sharing on your blog alongside what you are already talking about elsewhere online so that when you are sharing your blog content, it ties into everything else. For example, say you have been talking about a new Instagram marketing strategy all week long, write a blog post about that so that you already have a leg up when it comes to sharing your post because people have grown used to hearing you talk about it all week long. The more you work these types of long-term strategies into your promotional practices, the more your strategy will work because you are putting in the work of becoming known rather than just seen. This is the big difference between those who grow and those who do not: those who grow do not just want their content seen; they want their content remembered and revisited regularly. This is how they stay in the minds of their audience and continue to grow their blogs over time, by really making an impact and being memorable.

Integrating Your Blog with Your Audio and Visual Content

If you have a podcast, YouTube channel, or both, integrating these with your blog is an excellent way to cross-promote while also giving you even more content to talk about. A great example of people who integrate their blogs with their audio or visual content includes Amanda Frances and Jess Lively. Amanda Frances uploads a new blog every Wednesday that has a YouTube video that is followed by the video that has been transcribed so that people can either watch, listen to, or read the content that she is sharing depending on what interests them. Frances also recently started a podcast that she also shares in her blog, again giving people the capacity to either read or listen to her latest content. Jess Lively does the same by uploading her podcast links into her blog and writing a short excerpt about each podcast episode so that people can go to her blog, get an idea for what each episode entails, and then watch it. This is a great opportunity to cross-promote, while also gaining the SEO benefits of a blog, and keeping your audio or visual content all housed together in one simple-to-find area on your website. For many people, this is the easiest way to group audio or visual content on your website, as it is all in the same location and can easily be searched by your audience.

If you have a podcast or YouTube channel and you do not necessarily want to start a blog, but you do want the benefits of having one, you can always use your blog exclusively for sharing your audio or visual content. You do not necessarily need to transcribe your videos or offer any other type of content, but instead, you can simply leave the short excerpts of your posts combined with your podcasts.

You can always do the alternative with a podcast or YouTube channel to a blog as well, where you may make one, or several, smaller videos or podcasts with individual points from a blog post and then link each video or podcast back to a blog post that has far more in-depth information. This is another great opportunity to draw your audience back to your blog, and draw your blog audience out to your podcast or YouTube channel, allowing you to promote everything equally—thus growing your platform even faster.

Marketing Your Blog Effectively

Lastly, make sure that you are marketing your blog effectively, as nothing is worse than having a great blog post and a poor marketing strategy that does not do your blog justice. Your marketing strategy should be just as thought out as your posting strategy when it comes to finding new content for you to write about. You want to ensure that you are paying attention to how social media algorithms work on the platforms that you are sharing on, and that you are learning how to generate posts that get your content seen by your audience. Pay attention to how you can use keywords, when you should be posting, how long your posts should be, and what hashtags you should be using if you should be using any on that platform. The clearer you are on how each platform works when it comes to marketing, the easier it is going to be for you to write marketing posts for your blogs that are going to get your blogs seen. In other words: do not just drop a link and jet off, or write a poorly crafted post that does not get any eyes turned on your blog, as this is going to waste your time and cause your blog to grow extremely slowly.

In addition to learning how to write your marketing posts on these other social media platforms successfully, make sure that you are leveraging them effectively in general. For example, most social media platforms thrive when you share 20 percent marketing content and 80 percent of other content, so if you want to be sharing your blog posts on social media platforms, you also need to be sharing other content on those platforms so that you actually get seen. This way, you are leveraging these platforms and getting far more eyes on your profile, making it easier for you to get your blog posts seen in the first place.

When it comes to marketing your blog or website in general, you should always see the process as a sales funnel. Even if you are not selling anything on each blog post, you want to view it in this way so that you can make sense of how the content is working on getting people to your page. Your sales funnel works by having people find you on social media and fall in love with your social media presence, then click through to your website where they can gain more value from the content that you share there. Once they are there, and they fall in love, you can then use the content on your page to eventually drive your audience to your sales pages where they can sign up for your programs, buy your products, or otherwise purchase from you. If you are working as an influencer, you will use your blog posts to then send people to the website of the company you are promoting so that your audience can purchase their products or services—thus earning you a commission.

Conclusion

Congratulations on completing *Personal Branding: How to Brand Yourself Online in 2019 Using Social Media Marketing and the Hidden Potential of Instagram Influencers, Facebook Advertising, YouTube, Twitter, Blogging, and More!*

This book should have shown you how to leverage some of the most popular internet tools to grow your personal brand and make an income online. This book was designed to help you first clarify and grow your personal brand so that you can easily know what it is that you are aiming to market to your audience. This way, you can feel confident that your audience is going to know who you are because *you* know who you are. After clarifying your brand, you were shown how to influence major platforms to grow your brand and get in front of your audience more to make an impact.

As you read through this book, hopefully, you began looking for ways to immediately apply the information and grow your brand. All the steps provided offered an opportunity to get yourself discovered so that you can grow your brand even further. The more you grow your brand, the more you are going to open yourself up to receiving opportunities through your brand that will allow you to keep growing and make a profit. The key here is to understand that the application of the tools provided in this book needs to be consistent to gain value from them, so do not feel like you are failing or your brand is not good enough simply because you do not get instant results. When it comes to personal branding, your ability to stay consistent and out there is a large part of your ability to get seen and heard.

In addition to being consistent, you also need to make sure that you are being smart and approaching your brand as a business, even if you are not making a profit from it yet. The more you get to know your brand, the more you will understand what it takes to grow it, but you will only get to that point if you take the time to get to know your brand. This means that you need to pay attention to how people interact with you, what your metrics are and what they say about your brand, and how effectively you are enforcing your marketing strategies.

The next step is to implement these strategies. You also need to make a commitment to yourself and your brand that you are going to continue implementing and refining these strategies for a set period (say, six months) so that you can see the value they bring. You *will not* see growth from your brand if you do not stay committed to your new strategies, or if you do not stay committed to seeing how they can fit into your brand. Do not do yourself the disservice of being too loose with your goals, as this will result in your failure.

Lastly, if you enjoyed this book, an honest review on Amazon Kindle is always appreciated.

Best of luck!

Check out another book by Matt Golden

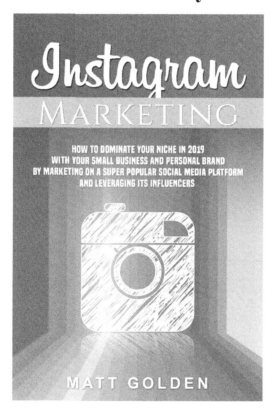

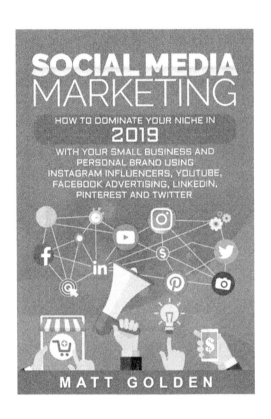

Printed in Great Britain
by Amazon

18585345R00058